£7.95

THE QUALITY OF WRITING

Open University Press
English, Language, and Education series

General Editor: Anthony Adams
Lecturer in Education, University of Cambridge

This series is concerned with all aspects of language in education from the primary school to the tertiary sector. Its authors are experienced educators who examine both principles and practice of English subject teaching and language across the curriculum in the context of current educational and societal developments.

TITLES IN THE SERIES

Computers and Literacy
Daniel Chandler and Stephen Marcus (eds.)

Children Talk About Books: Seeing Themselves as Readers
Donald Fry

The English Department in a Changing World
Richard Knott

Teaching Literature for Examinations
Robert Protherough

Developing Response to Fiction
Robert Protherough

Microcomputers and the Language Arts
Brent Robinson

The Quality of Writing
Andrew Wilkinson

The Writing of Writing
Andrew Wilkinson (ed.)

In preparation

EnglishTeaching: Programme and Policies
Anthony Adams and Esmor Jones

Literary Theory and English Teaching
Peter Griffith

THE QUALITY OF WRITING

Andrew Wilkinson

With contributions by
SALLY PARAMOUR
and
GILLIAN WORSLEY

Open University Press

Milton Keynes · *Philadelphia*

Open University Press
Open University Educational Enterprises Limited
12 Cofferidge Close
Stony Stratford
Milton Keynes MK11 1BY, England

and
242 Cherry Street
Philadelphia, PA 19106, USA

First published 1986

British Library Cataloguing in Publication Data

Wilkinson, Andrew M.
  The quality of writing.

  (English, language, and education series)
  Bibliography: p.
  Includes index.
  1. English language—Composition and exercises.
2. Language arts (Elementary)   I. Paramour, Sally.
II. Worsley, Gillian.   III. Title.   IV. Series.
LB1576.W4877   1985   372.6   85–29774

ISBN 0–335–15229–5

Library of Congress Cataloging in Publication Data

Wilkinson, Andrew
  The quality of writing.—(English, language,
  and education series)
  1. Language arts   2. English language—
  writing
  I. Title.   II. Series
  808'.042   P51

ISBN 0–335–15229–5

Text design by Clarke Williams
Typeset by S & S Press, Abingdon, Oxfordshire
Printed in Great Britain at the Alden Press, Oxford

this book is for
María Isabel León P.
Catherine Isabel Victoria

Contents

Acknowledgements

I should like to acknowledge with gratitude the help of many friends and fellow students who have been working with me in one capacity or another over the past five years mainly at the University of East Anglia.

Particular thanks go to Sally Paramour, who is the principal author of Chapters 9 and 10, and Gillian Worsley, whose work is mainly presented in Chapters 5 and 6. A study by Redmond Curtis for the Atlantic Institute, Halifax, Nova Scotia, contributed to the revision of the affective model. Anne Bauers has helped considerably by welcoming research in the school of which she is head, Wrentham Primary School, Beccles, Suffolk. Invaluable samples of writing have been provided by James Bidwell, June Kell, Bettina Kulsdom, Hilary Martins, Sarah Moore, Sarah Scurfield, and John Wallace-Jones in their researches into the implications of the Crediton Project. Members of the MA and Advanced Certificate Language in Education courses in the University, 1984–85 (J. Bidwell, G. Coneys, W. Foot, B. Kulsdom, A. Littlefair, D. Metson, C. Onwere, H. Pearson, F. Rimmell, E. Watkins, J. Robinshaw, E. Wilcock, M. Vigar), provided much valuable comment and feedback on aspects of the work, particularly its classroom implications, and this is presented in the Appendix. In this connection I wish to thank the East Anglian Examinations Board and Erik Wilcock for permission to reproduce his Airport Simulation in the Appendix. An earlier version of Chapter I appeared in *Educational Review* 37(1); of Chapter 2 and Chapter 9 in *Language Arts* 60(7) and 62(4) respectively; and acknowledgements are extended to the Editors of these journals.

I especially wish to thank my Secretary, Eileen Chapman. Her organising, planning, and secretarial skills have made her an essential complement to the research enterprises. She is also the only person in the UK who can ready my handwriting.

Andrew M. Wilkinson
Norwich, September 1985

General Editor's Introduction

The name of Professor Andrew Wilkinson is unlikely to need any introduction to readers of this book. Professor Wilkinson's earliest seminal work was, of course, in the field of oracy (a term which he coined on the analogy with literacy) and it is a matter of considerable importance that he has in recent years turned his attention to the field of writing. (His very influential book, 'The Foundations of Language', Oxford University Press, 1971, dealt amongst other things, with early reading, so that, in the total corpus of his work, Professor Wilkinson has covered all of the main language modes).

His interest in writing was first demonstrated in print in 'Assessing Children's Language', Oxford University Press, 1980, which was based upon the now well-known 'Crediton Project', a piece of research conducted when he held the Chair of Education at the University of Exeter. It was a desire to know more about what had happened subsequently to Crediton that led me to suggest to Professor Wilkinson that he might contribute to this series. (Those familiar with the Crediton Project will find the Appendix entitled 'Crediton in the Classroom' of particular interest in showing how research can lead directly into the production of classroom materials).

What has emerged is something much more significant than we had anticipated. 'The Quality of Writing' includes a highly readable survey of a vast field, as well as an account of original research. The account of research into writing in Chapter 3 does justice to a great deal of material in its 20 odd pages. I was especially pleased to see the attention paid to work of Philip Hartog, and the challenges to many of the accepted views about writing. In the last 10 years an orthodoxy of view about the writing process has developed ; it is characteristic of Wilkinson that he refuses to accept the received view of other authorities but argues cogently and, on the basis of sound evidence, for a view of his own. One example of this is his casting doubts upon the value of children's revisions or successive drafts of their own texts.

A feature of Wilkinson's work is his extensive quoting from students' work. A major concern throughout the book is the element of 'affect' in children's writing and a sense and capacity for feeling (alongside intellectual acumen) is the major impression that the reader takes away from the book as a whole.

It is not often that a report of academic research has so personal a note about it. It has its own internal narrative flow that carries its readers along so that most of them may ignore the author's helpful section entitled 'How to Read this Book' which sends them to the particular pages dealing with their main concerns. In my own reading I found particularly telling those moments in the text when Wilkinson illustrates his points by reference to works of literature.

In spring 1985 Professor Wilkinson organised the first of a series of biennial conferences to be held at the University of East Anglia. Some of the papers from this conference are also being published in this Open University Press series under the title, 'The Writing of Writing', edited by Andrew Wilkinson. The two books, taken together, provide as good a picture as is possible of the current state of research into writing. Severally, or together, they make a major contribution to our thinking.

It may have been forgotten these days, except by his many friends, that Andrew Wilkinson has some years ago an alter ego, Peter Gurney, the writer of radio plays, under which name he won the prized Italia Award. It is fitting that a writer on 'The Quality of Writing' should himself be a writer of quality. In the case of Wilkinson and this book, this is certainly the case. I wish the purchaser enjoyable reading.

Anthony Adams

Introduction

What this book is about

It is sometimes said that certain politicians are ready to sell their grand-mothers for political advantage.

It is not our purpose to consider whether this is true or not, but rather to regard it as a subject for writing. Writers would have to decide how to treat it, and some of their most important decisions would be as follows.

There would have to be a choice of the form in which to write — whether an article for a 'quality' paper about standards in public life; or a story for one of the 'popular' papers emphasising the scandal surrounding a named individual ('Super-Gran Salesman Charged'); or, at a less superficial level, a work of fiction, a short story, say, or a novel, which explores a particular — real or imaginary — incident. And the choice of form would require a certain organisation of the material, selection of certain vocabulary and types of sentence, which would be influenced by the readers in mind. (Popular papers assume their readers can only cope with simple sentences.) Choices of this kind are choices of *style*.

Also there would be choices of intellectual treatment; whether there should be, for example, merely a presentation of information, or whether there should be an attempt to interpret it, analyse it, consider its implications. Not all these choices are conscious, and not all writers would be able to carry them out with the same degree of insight because, sad to say, some writers are more stupid than others. Choices of this kind are *cognitive* choices.

Again the writer would have to choose, particularly if a story form had been decided upon, how to portray the people concerned. Is the politician disturbed by his action, or does he feel very little, telling himself one can't be too choosy in politics? Has he enough self-knowledge to know why he is behaving like this, and is he conscious of the image he is presenting to others? How does granny feel? Delighted at being able to help her grandson in this way? Or does she take a very selfish view of things, by refusing to cooperate and insisting on staying on in her cottage at Mumps Bridge,

Oldham. Choices of this kind, concerning the feelings, are *affective* matters.

And yet again the writer would indicate, whether explicitly or implicitly, a view of the politician's actions. In a novel, for example, a whole range of attitudes could be represented through the mouths of the characters, attitudes which can be classified. 'She's his granny, so why not,' (expediency); 'She should cut him from her will' (virtue rewarded, vice punished); 'It's not really *nice* — people don't like that sort of thing' (social approval/disapproval); 'The law won't allow it' (institutional morality); 'It's not his fault; he didn't want to, his grandad made him' (judgement by intention and motivation). Some people would simply say: 'It's just wrong — you can't sell human beings', which is a judgement in terms of right and wrong. Clearly such judgements and the preference the writer expresses are *moral* matters.

We have mentioned then, the stylistic, the cognitive, the affective, and the moral aspects of writing. These will be explained much more fully later, but they are what the book is about. In the past there has often been a tendency to consider writing in terms of the first only. But we take a more comprehensive view and examine also the nature of the thought, of the feeling and of the moral stance. It is all these things which make up the 'quality of writing' which is thus the title of this book.

This approach was pioneered in the University of Exeter (Wilkinson and Wilkinson, 1978) and the first major research (Wilkinson, Barnsley, Hanna and Swan, 1980) became known as the Crediton Project. A knowledge of the Project is essential for the advanced student. It is, however, not necessary for the general reader of this book, which is based on work carried out since then at the University of East Anglia and elsewhere, the findings of the Crediton Project being summarised as appropriate.

How to read this book

If you have no knowledge of the approach set out in the previous section read Chapter 2 for a summary of the Crediton Project. Follow this by reading Chapter 11, 'Assessment of written composition' and 'An assessment scheme for written composition', for more details about assessing compositions by the Crediton 'models'.

Then you will be in a position, with more experienced readers, to make a choice of further reading. If you want to follow up work on 'affect', read Chapter 7, concerning writers' responses to themselves and others; and Chapter 8, concerning their attitudes to the non-human world. Chapter 6 concerns their attitudes to the problems and challenges of life. If you want to follow up work on cognition, read Chapter 4, which emphasises the importance of writing for the development of our thinking. If your interest is in style, read Chapters 9 and 10, which are specially concerned with narrative as an aspect of style. If you seek work on moral attitudes in writing you are unlucky. There are only 48 hours any one day, and we have been unable to carry out further work on this topic since the Crediton Project.

For readers seeking a rationale for the approach, Chapters 1 and 5 are essential, and considerably advance the tentative argument of the original Project. Chapter 3 places our studies in the context of a review of writing-research this century. For readers seeking the curriculum implications of the approach, Chapter 1 and the Appendix will be of interest.

But you certainly ought to read Chapter 12. It will not detain you long, being perhaps one of the shortest chapters ever written, but gets you to the heart of the matter.

1   I write therefore I am

Writing and Creating

To speak is to write on water. Our words make no mark on the colourless surface, and are swept away immediately. If we wish to consider the words we have spoken we must make black marks on a white page. This is an important difference between speech and writing. Writing can help us more to consider our thoughts, to analyse our feelings, because it gives us time to do so. In a way it serves the function of a mirror enabling us to reflect on ourselves and thus to make changes, just as a woman may become more beautiful before the make-up glass. In a sense we create ourselves — *I write, therefore I am.*

Writing, however, is only one form of communication. A communication informs, of course, but it also creates. We should really say *I communicate, therefore I am.* But different forms of communication create in different ways. The purpose of this chapter is to try to distinguish the special contribution of writing. To do this we shall try to explain the general statement *I communicate therefore I am* as a preliminary to considering the more specific *I write therefore I am.*

I communicate therefore I am

This proposition means, clearly, not that I exist physically, but that I exist as a personality, as a social being, with a self-image and identity in the social world. The proposition is only the first term of the paradigm. It is followed by *I communicate therefore you are* (and its converse) and by *I communicate therefore it is*, i.e. I create the universe in which I live.

    I communicate therefore I am
    I communicate therefore you are
    I communicate therefore it is

There are three basic communication models, and only three: transmission, reciprocity, reflection.

The simplest model is one in which information is passed from A to B — *a speaker addresses an audience, the media transmit, the actors perform, a writer writes a book. In the crudest manifestations B cannot contribute to what A is saying.* Least crude is perhaps an actor sensing the mood of an audience or a teacher grasping the learning difficulties of a class. This we call a transmission model.

A second model of communication is the reciprocal. In this model A communicates to B communicates to A communicates to B communicates to A, and so on. The second model of communication must of course comprehend the first. This is in fact the normal model in human relationships. Its basic description is 'conversation' — whether this be adult-child interaction, gossip, love talk — any situation in which there is an exchange.

A feature of this reciprocity is that the communication of A to some extent creates the communication of B creates the communication of A and thus to some extent A creates B creates A. If, for instance, A asks B a question he tends to determine that B will give him some sort of answer, and the meaning of the answer is prescribed in terms of the prompt or even the alternatives offered by the question.

The three communication models

Thus the two communication models are: AB and ABA. But there is a third which is reflective: $A\,A$. A communicates with A; A communicates with self, and this is very important indeed.

Model AB: Transmission
What does the first model tell us about the proposition: *I communicate therefore I am*? It tells us that we can inform, and regulate (influence, affect) other people. In other words it gives us a sense of being a source — a source of something — information, emotion, power. Even a young baby, before the age of language, knows this by the effect of various cries. They mean, whatever, their individual connotation, I am a force to be reckoned with. It is this model which underlies what has become known, in Goffman's terms, as 'the presentation of self' (Goffman, 1969).

So AB is assertion of being on the one hand, and regulation of other things on the other. In terms of assertion it is an attempt at self-definition — 'I am the greatest', for example — but ultimately without social verification it is meaningless. In terms of regulation it works with objects as an absolute — lifting a weight, moving a chair. With people it has to be socially conferred. If you are king of the castle it is ultimately because in some sense you are acknowledged to be so. Of course the acknowledgement which preserves a democratic ruler is different from that which preserves a tyrant. Power is one of the things which compels acknowledgement.

As a paradigm of *AB* we may take the classical teacher–taught relationship — what Barnes (1976) calls 'transmission'. The teacher transmits and the student receives. The research evidence is that teachers talk much more of the time in most lessons. Much of the information transmitted in secondary school is at low level on a cognitive scale, encouraging assimilation rather than thought. Thus the London Writing Research Unit (Britton *et al.*, 1975) found in secondary schools a high percentage of what is called low level 'transactional' writing — recording, reporting — much of which was dictated or copied. The DES (1979, p. 83) Secondary School Survey found the same. The self-statements of the teacher are inseparable from their regulatory roles, in which two types of activity are present — a teaching and a control function. Often the same language does both jobs: 'Get out your books and read quietly till the end of the period' for example. Sometimes there is a distinct control language. In first school it has been wittily observed by King (1979). Thus the teacher 'wishes aloud': 'I hope nobody is going to spoil our lovely story'. She refers to the headteacher:

> Now nice and quietly down the corridor.
> You know Mrs. Brown does not like noisy children.

She makes a general observation, apparently directed at no one in particular:

> Someone's being silly.

And so on. But however oblique the control, there is no question who is doing the controlling.

On the whole, then, the contribution of the model *AB* to the proposition *I communicate, therefore I am* is confined to the first clause — *I communicate*. Validation is by no means necessarily provided by the class response — it could come from training, past employment, DES certification. We must turn, therefore, to an examination of the second, the *ABA* model. This is, of course, the reciprocal model. In the *AB* model where feedback takes place at all it is often at a low level, as with a passive class, or at a great distance filtered indirectly, as with a TV programme or a novel. In the *ABA* model it is immediate, close, and continuous. Of course *ABA* also includes *AB*.

Model ABA: Reciprocity

As mentioned above, the prototype of *ABA* is conversation, and there are allied forms such as discussions, seminars, commercial transactions, disputations, and travesties of the interaction process such as committee meetings.

In conversation *A* makes a speech act to *B*. Whatever the speech act is it is in some sense creating *B*. If *A* asks a question *B* is created as an answerer, if he makes an unquestionable statement B is created as an agreer, or a commentor, and so on. But by the same token B is also creating A by the type of responses A makes. However, at the affective level something else is going on. B's responses are offering perceptions of A as a person. Approvals, agreements, favourable responses, including non-verbal ones such as smiles, nods and grunts, are enhancing of self-image. (In the same way praise rather than criticism is thought of as motivating learning in schoolchildren.) As a result of B's feedback A is created as (say) a kinder more intelligent person in A's own eyes; but also in fact may become so as a result of B's perceptions. The exchange theory of the sociologists comments on this dyad relationship in terms of four basic concepts — reward, cost, outcome and comparison level. The reward is what I am concerned with — in one sense I am seeking a definition of myself by means of a conversation. I would not say 'I am good at telling jokes, aren't I?'; rather I would make a witty remark and be rewarded by a smile. If then I made many such remarks and only received an occasional smile then the 'cost' would have outrun the rewards, resulting in a negative 'outcome', though here the 'comparison level' is relevant — if A had never even succeeded in amusing B at all and now received one smile the overall 'outcome' would be positive (Secord and Blackman, 1974), pp. 222–3).

This dyad relationship and the reward it offers on a particular occasion is only a tiny example of how A communicated a question and received an answer. In terms of social roles A often does not need to ask. The knowledge of the role is often enough for others to make a statement defining it — in for instance, as the most obvious form, modes of address, but also in a well-described range of non-verbal communication. Attitudes of deference towards a boss, or statements of social superiority, for example, are often noted in the literature. 'Employment' in itself is a key status conferrer, as we have had reason to observe only too ruefully in recent years. With women who do not work for family reasons the question 'what do you do?' in casual conversation often reveals a miserably embarrassed 'nothing'.

Personality is partly built up by the use of language to obtain reflections,

> Mirror mirror on the wall
> who is the fairest of us all

partly, by conferment, not only *I communicate, therefore I am*, but *I communicate, therefore you are*.

We may take one example of the ABA relationship which seems to make it particularly meaningful, even poignant — an aspect of 'intersubjectivity'.

Intersubjectivity. The term is Trevarthen's. He is concerned with very young infants, and the great complexity of the genetically-based behavioural systems with which they are endowed. As Newson and Newson (1975, p. 441) say:

> He seems inclined to stress the inborn nature of the ability to take part in complex social interaction rituals, and he describes the phenomenon as 'innate intersubjectivity': when Trevarthen uses the terms 'intersubjectivity' he is referring to a specific kind of sociability which mediates communication between human to human subjects. It is his view that infants are inherently responsive to those patterns of temporal movements which typically govern the episodic behaviour cycles of most living organisms.

The rhythms of the human race seem to call forth precisely synchronised motor movements in new-born babies. Thus babies seem to be natural conversationalists — looking attentive on being spoken to, waiting for an appropriate pause before responding. Since 'the baby plays a very active and self-directing role from the outset, the course of the ensuing dialogue is never strictly under the sole control of either partner'. (p. 442). Clearly intersubjectivity is the *ABA* model. Let us look first at the *AB* relationship, and then later at the *BA* relationship.

From *A* to *B* there is transmission – but we shall use instead the term *conferment* because transmission may imply the passing of factual information only, and we are concerned with a whole complex of cognitive and affective factors. To the baby physical presence says 'you are not alone'; physical contact says 'you are safe as in the hand of God'. Presence, voice, touch, smell convey security, just as the breast conveys sustenance. Other things are conferred because the baby can imitate very early. If you pull your tongue out at a baby of two months it is likely to respond likewise. At the same age babies make grunting, honking, bubble-and-squeak noises which they have not copied, but within the next month they may be, as it were, 'joining in' conversations, when adults are talking. What has been conferred to them already is the information that talking happens, and that they have a part to play.

What seems to be pre-programmed is the preference for speech or speech-like sounds over other sounds. And of course the babies respond to being talked to directly by making noises and often waving their arms and legs about excitedly at the same time. This is not surprising because it is exactly what adults do, though less obviously. And certainly the baby develops the skill of turn-taking. Babies of three months often 'talk' at the same time as the adult is talking to them, but are learning to take turns. Some adults after all never learn.

A second form of conferment is that the parents treat the babies as if they were other than they are, as if their behaviour had adult significance. An early facial gesture is seized on as a smile, is smiled back at, a smile which is imitated by the baby and thus reinforced at the time in a context of relaxation and enjoyment.

Let us turn to the other *ABA* relationship, *BA*.

There is also *BA* conferment. For instance in the very important matter of speech. It used to be thought that 'baby talk' was contrived by parents as a means of enjoying their own regressions. Chomskyian theory anyway did not require it — you only had to be exposed to comparatively few fragments of language to acquire the whole rule-system. However, 'baby talk', dignified by the abbreviation BT, is now being claimed as one of a simplified set of universal registers used to people felt unable to understand normal adult speech, and which has 100 or more lexical, grammatical, and phonological features. It has the functions of simplifying, clarifying, and expressing (creating affect). What part does the baby play in all this?

One feature certainly is the baby's preference for the human faces (Haaf and Bell, 1967). The directness of their gaze may be related to the face-making behaviour we see in adults when dealing with small babies. And this directness may again account for the repetition which is so much a feature of BT; the child not having learnt to give the nods and grunts which are a feature of adult feedback. (Gleason, 1977, pp. 199–205). Again the baby's non-response prompts the adult to supply both sides of the conversation—question and answer for example.

More important, however, than these conferments is the conferment of value. The baby is conferring motherhood on the mother, for instance. Responses such as eye contact, smiles, are felt by the mother as granting special favour; they seem to signal love, and prompt the growth of love. As Wills (1977) writes:

> 'Devotion' is not automatic. For the mother of a sighted baby her love for her child, whatever its admixtures, is developed and cemented by the pleasurable interaction between herself and the child, in which visual interchange plays a very great role. The mother can understand the child on the basis of her own sensory experience and so is soon responding to him meaningfully, and this gives her not only pleasure in the relationship but a feeling of value as a mother.

How important such conferment is can be noted with reference to blindness. Wills goes on:

> The mother of a blind child, however, at a time when she is sad and disappointed, is confronted by a passive baby whose responses to her overtures are by no means obvious: e.g. he may become still and silent when she comes to pick him up in order to *listen* to her approach, not smiling and cooing like a sighted infant who can see her approach.

This apparent lack of response may be felt as rejection by the mother which may in certain cases cause her to reject the child. More extreme disabilities produce a greater incidence of rejection.

Model AA: Reflection

So far we have looked at the communication models *AB* and *ABA*, that is, without feedback, and with feedback from significant others. Let us now look at the third model, AA, the model with the self as recipient of the message.

We take it that the prime example of this is thought itself — the dialogue inside the head — the interminable conversation with its questions and answers. Idiomatic expressions in our language show that this is well recognised — 'I said to myself', 'I asked myself the question', for instance. This dialogue is perpetually concerned with three basic questions: Who am I? What do I think? What do I feel? The first is concerned with self-image and body-image; the second with the assertion, examination, revision of our propositions; the third with feelings and attitudes.

In the world outside the head these processes, it would seem, are best represented in writing: there are so many examples to be taken from literature that it is necessary to be very selective and cursory. Let us take the first question: who am I? This is the subject of so many autobiographical novels. Instead I shall take a poem by Hegginbotham (1965) from the sequence *Mirror, Mirror*. The mirror is of course the prime symbol of AA dialogue. The poem is called 'Hall of Mirrors'.

> There was a hall of mirrors
> Some shape of me was in all mirrors
> But the hall itself was empty
>
> There was a hall of mirrors
> I was in the hall of mirrors
> But not in any of the mirrors
>
> To see myself I had to
> Look down at my body
> And peer cross-eyed down my nose
>
> This view shewed up a monster —
> a body without a head
> A nose without a face.

What comes out well, for our purpose, in this poem, is the position of the individual whose selfhood lacks external validation.

To turn to the second concern of the *AA* dialogue: what do I think? The relationship of thinking to writing and the ways in which thinking may be developed by writing is one of our major preoccupations at the present time. The suggestion is that it can be the most important means of educating thinking, for writing enables us to try out concepts and consider their relations in a way which is impossible in speech.

The third concern of the *AA* dialogue is: what do I feel? This is often best represented, certainly best-examined, in writing, where, as Justin (13) says,

I try to think from to minds as though I was two people.

These three are concerns the original Crediton Project took up, and which form the substance of this book.

I write therefore I am

We have suggested that writing is a prime means of developing the thinking, and the emotions, and of defining (and redefining) ourselves. The simple reason for this is that it gives us the time and the opportunity for reflection — time because the words are not gone as soon as uttered, opportunity because they are fixed before us on the page so that we can consider them.

Thinking on paper is characterised by an ability to record the factors involved, to classify or otherwise order them, to observe the connections between them, to draw conclusions from them, all the time going backwards and forwards over them to reconsider, to modify, add or subtract additional information. As Bacon wryly said: 'If a man write little, he had need have a great memory'. Speech, of course, carries abstractions, but people who want to present an extended abstract argument so often resort to writing. Speech, of course can produce ideas, in, for instance, conversation or discussion, but often the ideas are not evaluated: I'll have to go away and think about it', people say — 'weigh and consider' in Bacon's phrase. Speech, of course, can revise; we can say 'What I meant to say was . . .'; but we can't keep on doing this — discussion has to flow, and constant repetitions and apologies become tedious. In contrast revisions, second thoughts, are easy in writing, and nobody knows the result until the writer is satisfied. Speech can concentrate, of course, but the span of attention of listeners is limited; and anyway speech is doing so much else — presenting the speaker as a person, maintaining social relations in a group, and so on. Speech, of course, can be exact, though much idiom in ordinary conversation is emotive rather than exact. It can be used to blur or avoid issues, as our smooth politicians know, but, significantly enough, their speeches are often *written* for them beforehand to make sure the exact degree of inexactness is present. As Bacon again said: 'Reading maketh a full man, conference a ready man, and writing an exact man' (Bacon, 1876, p. 501).

Feeling on paper has many of the characteristics of thinking on paper — the ability to consider and reconsider, to research for exactness. But the objects of concern will be different: the writer will often be considering the question — what do I really feel? and so will be concerned with attitudes and motives — of the self, of others, towards the environment, and towards the problems of life in general. The writing process is one in which writers often work their way towards unique statements on these matters, perhaps through a series of drafts, or alterations of individual words. We could take countless illustrations from the drafts of published writers. Let us confine ourselves to two.

In Dylan Thomas's papers after his death were found his manuscripts of the poem 'Elegy'. It was concerned with the death of his father. For one of the verses he seems to have started with a note:

> Although he was too proud to die, he *did* die, blind
> in the most agonising way, but he did not flinch
> from death and was brave in his pride.

Eventually the first verse of the poem became:

> Too proud to die, broken and blind he died
> The darkest way, and did not turn away,
> A cold kind man brave in his narrow pride.

The lines are tightened up — the omission of the first three words emphasises the starkness of the paradox that he died although too proud to do so: the phrase 'The darkest way' brings out at once the blindness and the agony, dispensing with the more prosaic 'in the most agonising way'; the part abstract 'did not flinch from death' is replaced by the concrete 'did not turn away'. His finest substitution is the last line which brings out the austerity and humanity, the nobility in the egotism. Here Thomas moves from an interesting and adequate statement to a brilliant characterisation. It is not reported how many versions he made of this particular verse; but we do know that there were sixty pages of manuscripts to the poem which was only part finished at his death. (Thomas, 1967, pp. 179–82).

A second illustration is provided by the two versions of Wordsworth *Prelude*, the first published in 1805, the second, revised, version in 1850. In the second version many see the older Wordsworth asking himself the question, what do I really feel *now*? Even a few lines can begin to give us the different flavour. In the 1805 version we read:

> Oh there is blessing in this gentle breeze
> That blows from the green fields and from the clouds
> And from the Sky; it beats against my cheek
> And seems half conscious of the joy it gives.

In the 1850 version this becomes:

> O there is blessing in this gentle breeze,
> A visitant that while it fans my cheek
> Doth seem half conscious of the joy it brings
> From the green fields and from yon azure sky.

There is much more exuberance in the earlier version. For instance, the breeze 'blows' in the first version and 'beats against my cheek', whereas in the second it merely 'fans my cheek'. The earlier version goes on:

> A welcome Messenger, O welcome friend!
> A captive greets thee, coming from a house
> Of bondage, from yon City walls set free,
> A prison where he had been long immured.
> Now I am free, enfranchis'd and at large.
> May fix my habitation where I will.

But the older Wordsworth is no longer sure that the breeze is such a clear symbol. Nor does he regard the city as a prison — his is a more cautious description — in the later version he has been a 'discontented sojourner there':

> Whate'er its mission, the soft breeze can come
> To none more grateful than to me: escaped
> From the vast city, where I long had pined
> A discontented sojourner; now free,
> Free as a bird to settle where I will.

The difference is rather like that between someone who has been re-leased from Wormwood Scrubs after a long prison sentence, and someone who is retiring from a boring city job and a bedsitter in Earls Court. In fact the younger Wordsworth had just heard he had received a legacy of £900 (perhaps equivalent to £90,000 today): the older Wordsworth might have felt similarly ecstatic in the circumstances.

The third feature of the *AA* dialogue that we have mentioned is the defining and redefining of the self. It is of course an obsessive concern of adolescence in which the 'identity crisis', the establishment of the self as a distinct individual from parents, is most acute. But the process never ceases because roles and circumstances change. Of course the self is to some extent socially conferred — *you communicate therefore I am*, as we saw earlier in the chapter. Our feeling of worth may be altered by the appreciations or depreciations of others. On the other hand others, and the world without, are to some extent our creation: *I communicate therefore you are; I communicate therefore it is*. It is here, in the opportunity to take stock, to assess human dignity, that the *AA* dialogue may be important; and may be particularly important for many people through writing. The grey soul contemplates the white page and in that mirror learns understandings: 'I write therefore I am'.

Comment

This chapter has emphasised the special role of writing in refining our thinking and feeling, and in defining ourselves. Writing does this because it causes us to reflect in what we have called the *AA* dialogue. But John (14) puts it much more simply:

> Trying to assess myself gives me a headache. It's as though you're having a fight, but its inside your head . . .

2 The development of writing

The Crediton Project

A good deal is known about how children acquire oral language before starting school, and there is a fair measure of agreement about their stages of growing competence with its forms.

After that, however, little is known. Take writing, for instance. It was easy for the old textbook writers. They assumed that English developed in 'stages'. So they choose their series title ('The Path to Glory'), and called the volumes Stage One, Stage Two, and so on). However English is not a linear subject, and a person's language abilities are complex, so that progress is not really like climbing a ladder from one rung to the next. It is less misleading to think of it as the waves advancing and retreating on a beach, one wave making a gain but the next falling short of it, just as a young writer may present very variable quality of work from one week to the next. Obviously over a period progress is taking place, but is not taking place obviously.

We all have our intuitions about the nature of this development; teachers might say 'Quite good for an eight-year-old' or 'You'd expect better than that at twelve', thus indicating that they possess expectations based on experience. But the characteristics on which these judgements are made are seldom examined. This was what a group of researchers working with teachers in their schools in Crediton, Devon, set out to do, in an investigation which became known as the Crediton Project. From this original project stems much of the work subsequently carried out at the University of East Anglia which is the basis of the present book. Hence this chapter is devoted to an outline of the Crediton Project, though an acquaintance with the original report (Wilkinson *et al.*, 1980) is necessary for fuller understanding. In its simplest form the Project may be described as an analysis of various types of composition produced by writers aged seven, ten and 13.

Obtaining the compositions
In studying the competence of a writer to use language it is no use taking

one example only. We are all aware of how we vary from situation to situation in our speech and writing. Skilled teachers have a broadly-based 'model of discourse' — that is to say they see to it that each pupil carries out a variety of tasks so that the different aspects of linguistic competence are required and developed. A common but uninformed view of primary teaching is that it emphasises 'creative writing' to the exclusion of other forms of writing. A common view of secondary schools, for which there is some evidence, is that they stress factual writing (particularly in the examination-dominated years) and require very little personal writing. Clearly in both cases the 'model of discourse' is far too narrowly based.

Within the limits of our resources it was not possible to take all the written work of the pupils we wished to study. Instead we had to select tasks which would be representative of pupils' abilities. The Assessment of Performance Unit, facing a similar problem, decided to choose tasks on four dimensions; narrative/descriptive or reflective/analytical; control by writer or tester (treatment fairly free or closely prescribed); first- or second-hand subject matter; literary or functional. This resulted in seven tasks for 11-year-olds, and eight for 15-year-olds. We selected tasks on the basis of function and reader. It seems sensible to choose tasks which would lead both to personal and to discursive writing, and to postulate readers in the school and known directly to the children. After various trials we chose four such tasks which also included the APU dimensions except that they all required first-hand subject matter.

The tasks — four compositions — two personal, two discursive — were as follows. One was a piece of autobiography — 'The happiest or saddest day of my life'. This is a well-tried title used by Schonell and Schonell (1948), notable for its success. For the adolescents the title was modified to 'The best/worst experiences I ever had'. The reader was assumed to be the class's normal teacher. Another composition was a fictional story; the pupil selects a picture from three, and the instruction is 'Write a story for which your picture is one of the illustrations'. The writers knew that the results would be seen by their peers either on the class noticeboard or in a class anthology, both normal devices in the schools used. The third composition was an argument on the topic 'Would it work if children came to school when they liked, and could do what they liked there?' with the peer group as readership. The fourth composition was an explanation. The intention was that the writer could speak with authority. The task was to explain how to play a game (once again a Schonell and Schonell topic). The reader was anyone who wished to learn the game.

The design of the project was simple. We took groups of pupils at seven, ten and 13 and elicited from all of them the four compositions just described. No sophisticated matching procedures were used to select the pupils. The schools were a secondary school and one of its primary feeder schools in a community of considerable stability; the children in the one school often had brothers and sisters in the other. Within these schools we needed good groups which were fairly comparable, and we relied on the professional knowledge of the teachers to provide these. We were thus able to compare like with like.

To meet possible criticisms that the written tasks were imposed and 'unnatural' we tried to make them such as normally occur in English lessons, linking them as closely as possible with the direct experience of the pupils. Our collaborating teachers required the compositions as part of normal classroom work over a period of three months. This we felt would minimise the possible Hawthorne effect in the sample (a difference brought about by the sheer fact that the subjects know they are involved in a research project) and the negative effect of 'examination backwash' on the children's understanding of the tasks themselves.

Assessing the compositions

Once we had obtained the compositions our task was to assess them, and here a major problem presented itself. The method of assessment chosen is related to one's belief about one's role as a teacher of language. If one seeks to develop only the 'skills' of writing then one chooses a marking scheme focusing on these. But if one believes one is concerned foremost with the growth of individuals for whom language is a means to that end, then one's scheme of assessment is conceived fundamentally to perceive that growth ('skills' and all) and to further it. This was our belief; and thus we sought such a scheme. Commonly used 'marking schemes' are at once far too narrow and far too vague. Certainly none of the schemes came anywhere near describing the development we had in mind.

Behind any attempt to pick out features of development there must be a hypothesis about human development. In physical matters this is usually easy — we expect a baby to walk from about 12 months onwards, not to rush around the ward on the day of its birth. In psychological matters it is less clear. Our attempt was as follows: human development is a movement from a world of instances to a world organised by mind; from dependence to autonomy; from convention to uniqueness; from subjectivity to objectivity; from ignorance to understanding; from self to neighbour as self. There is no 'end product' — 'maturity' is not a state which is finally attained; one does not arrive, one is continually arriving.

If we were to look at the writer as a developing being we felt we must be as comprehensive as possible and look at the quality of thought, of the feeling, and of the moral stance manifested in the writing, as well as at the style. Matters such as punctuation, spelling, grammatical correctness are of course important, but these are commonly marked anyway. We wanted to look at other ways of assessment.

Models of assessment

Hence four models were devised to serve as systems of analysis — in the fields of cognition, affect, morals and style. The complete models are printed in Wilkinson *et al.*, (1980). In summary they are as follows:

Cognitive. The basis of this model is a movement from an undifferentiated world to a world organised by mind, from a world of instances to a world related by generalities and abstractions.

Affective. Development is seen as being in four movement — one towards a greater awareness of self, a second towards a greater awareness of neighbour as self, a third towards a greater awareness of the non-human environment, and a fourth towards a stance towards the 'human condition'.

Moral. 'Anomy' or lawlessness gives way to 'heteronomy' or rule by fear of punishment, which in turn gives way to 'socionomy' or rule by a sense of reciprocity with others, which finally leads to the emergence of 'autonomy' or self-rule.

Stylistic. Development is seen as choices in relation to a norm of the simple literal affirmative sentence, which characterizes children's early writing. Features, such as structure, cohesion, verbal competence, syntax, reader awareness and appropriateness undergo modification.

It is not possible here to include the full models and demonstrate their application. However simplified models are set out in Table 1 which will serve to give some idea of the general dimensions.

Table 1: Simplified models based on Wikinson *et al.* (1980).

COGNITIVE

Overall	Describing	Interpreting	Generalising	Speculating
Detail	Simple facts, statements	Explanations and deductions	Summaries conclusions classifications	Substantial hypotheses, arguments, conclusions

AFFECTIVE

Self	Becoming aware — motives, context, image — of self
Self	Becoming aware of neighbour as self — of others
Self	Becoming aware of, celebrating, physical, social environment
Self	Coming to terms with the human condition — 'reality'

MORAL

Attitudes determined by	Physical characteristics or results	Rewards and punishments	Social approval	Conventional norms, laws	Motives	Abstract concepts

STYLISTIC

Organisation	Fragmentary, becomes more and more complete
Cohesion	Separate items (e.g. sentences) become cohesive
Syntax	Simple, complex, best suited for purpose
Lexis	General, unqualified uses become exact, chosen
Reader	Growing sense of reader's needs
Appropriateness	Movement into more acceptable/efficient mode

Assessment of autobiography

Let us look at the work of Peter, a seven-year-old writer in these terms:

> I got up from bed and in front of me was lods of parcels I opending them,
> And there was a England football kit. A ball a pair of football boots I was
> ever so happy. Then I went down stairs and thier was a huge dinner on the
> table then I rember it was my birthday I had a nother supise as well my anty
> came round for tea and she gave me three pounds and we had a tea party.
> I was ever to good that night so my mum let me stay up and watch match of
> the day then I went to bed that was the happest day of my life.

As far as the cognitive category is concerned this writing is *descriptive*. It
records a series of *facts* and *events* linked chronologically. In the affective
category it is egocentric and a statement about the satisfaction of needs of
the *self*. *Others* have no existence except as servicing agencies to the writer
— mum as a universal provider, aunty as a bearer of three pounds on one's
birthday. There is, not surprisingly, little reference to the physical *environment*, and the attitude towards *reality* is that it is completely under one's
control — as long as one is 'good'. In the moral category in fact the thinking is at quite a low level — that virtue is rewarded and vice punished.
That this is not universally true, needs no argument, but the assumption
is a convenient one fostered by parents and teachers in the furtherance of
efficient child-rearing and management.

   In stylistic terms the *organisation* is complete, but elementary — almost
entirely chronological. *Cohesion* is attained by simple connectives — *and,
but as well, so.* The syntax is predominantly simple sentences in form if not
in appearance. *Lexis* is general; adjectives and adverbs, for instance, have
a specifying function and there are scarcely any of these. We are seeing a
stage of word-use here which has two features. One feature is that the
words are multi-purpose — a few words can be used to do a large number
of jobs. Take the verbs, for example; nearly all of them are forms of 'be',
'have', 'got', 'go' — overwhelmingly the most common verbs in the language. At this age these multi-purpose verbs do not carry particular
shades of meaning. The other feature is that words used at this stage tend
to have single connotations derived from the context in which they were
learned; they have not been encountered in the contexts with different
connotations — for example dinner as an evening as well as a midday
meal. Though the list of events is a little monotonous there are the deliberate devices of 'rembering' and 'supise' to interest the reader. These are
devices from literature, showing movement towards 'appropriateness' in
written form, though the opening is very like speech.

   If we apply the same criteria to another writer's work on the same theme
we see some differences. Pauline is a year or so older than Peter (though
we are not saying that the differences are necessarily due to age):

I had just moved into a new house. I had no friends my sister was only about 4 years old I looked for some friends but I couldn't find any. Then I heard a noise someone was bouncing on a matrue then I looked over the wall and there I found somebody I said who are you? what is your name? she said the same to me it was my old friend I knew in play school (she is in this school now) she is called nicola Thorn. We played skipping until it was time for me to go in. I had my tea and I watched the television and I went to bed I said to myself I think that was the happiest day in my life. Nicola has been one of my Greatest friends right from that day. And she sometimes breaks with me but she soon comes running to me when she is my friend again.

Cognitively, Pauline gives us a descriptive narrative, but the most notable difference between her work and Peter's is that she *interprets* and *explains* — her opening isolation, for instance, is accounted for. In her last sentence she is moving towards a *generalisation* about friendship of the order of 'friendship can withstand shocks'. She is less egocentric than Peter in the sense that Nicola is a part of her happiness — it lies in an interaction, not merely an assertion of *self*. She can also look on herself externally: 'I said to myself . . .'. Awareness of the *other* is shown in the large amount of information we receive about her. There is no active relationship with the *environment*; but the sense of *reality* is more mature than Peter's, not all one long focus of adoration of the writer. People are lonely, quarrel, a happy state is not permanent, and no connection is made between this and *moral* deservings.

The *organisation* is interesting in that it is moving from chronology to narrative. Chronology gives us the relentlessness and undifferentiated march of events, almost entirely ordinary. Narrative selects and presents by interrupting and disrupting the ordinary (see Chapter 9). There is a chronology in Pauline's account. Had Peter been writing it, it would have begun at the noise, and finished with TV and bed. But Pauline inserts before it a retrospect so as to convey the necessary background; after it she brings us up to the present. Both these devices, and others, arise from a careful consideration of the needs of a *reader*, though there are features of the writing (asides, for instance) more usually felt to be appropriate in speech. The *lexis* is more differentiating — with a greater variety of verbs for instance — 'moved', 'heard', 'bouncing', 'played skipping', in addition to the basics. In *syntax* there is a greater variety of sentence though none complicated.

A third piece — by Jill, aged 11 — well demonstrates other features:

The best day of my life was at Barry Island. We were all staying at butilands holiday camp. It was the last day, we woke up to the sounds of the sea crashing against the rocks. My sister and me got up early and got dressed went into the kitchen and took some money and went out. We left a note for mum and dad to say gone to get the paper and to go along the sea front. We did not wake my brother up. When we got out it was a lovely day with the sun shining and a cool breeze. We went out of the camp site and down on to the sand. We took our sandles of and went in to the sea it was cold but refreshing. Then we played hit but it was not very good with just two of us. Then we wrote names in the sand. Then got the paper and came back when we got back everyone was up and we had breakfast then dad said Debras the greatest is she. He had seen what my sister wrote in the sand. Then we all went out and saw a really funny fight no one got hurt then we went and bought some presents and things and went on to the beach. Had our lunch in a restruant. Went back and packed our bags. Then went to the station. we did not want to go, we walked through the fair to the station. Got on the train which was crowed it was very hot. when we got back home we had tea unpacked and watched t.v. then we went to bed. When we got in bed my sister and me talked about the day.

Describing is the principle cognitive operation — an immense amount of information is given with explanation (the note) where necessary. In the affective area there are two new features. One is an awareness of the *other*, a realisation of his unique personality. Nicola Thorn was, as it were, a dependent of the writer with no real distinguishing features: but here 'dad' is brought alive as a personality in his own right, just in the single phrase he speaks we know what sort of person he is. The other is an awareness of the *environment*. Jill certainly illustrates it. *The moral* dimension is not explicit; the assumption is of a world in which responsibility to others is a norm.

Stylistic features are interesting. *Organisationally* a narrative is embedded within a chronology. From 'My sister and me' as far as 'He had seen what my sister wrote in the sand' is clearly a shaped whole, held by the device of withholding the information about what Debbie had written in the sand. In time, what she wrote and her writing it were simultaneous: here they are separated. The rest of the composition is conscientious reporting. The *syntax* is fairly simple — except that Jill demonstrates an ability to curtail it by leaving out subjects. Certain items of *lexis* are literary ('sun shining and a cool breeze'). It seems that children may need to attain to the conventional before gaining the individual. Otherwise, however, there is a great deal of very basic vocabulary (notice the verbs). There is still a strong element of oral language but there is a striving after written *appropriateness*. In the core story the *reader* is very skilfully handled; less so elsewhere.

The writing of a 13-year-old is likely to display characteristics not found earlier, as well as others that were foreshadowed. This is a piece by Nina:

It was just like any other Tuesday. Normal breakfast, normal lessons, little did I know that this was going to be one of the saddest days of my life.

I got off the bus as normal, walked up the hill, opened the gate, walked down the steps, pressed on the latch. Then, it was different.

My Mum opened the door, her eyes were red her cheeks puffed out, she'd obviously been crying. Bewildered, I asked 'What's happened?' Thoughts flashed through my mind, who's hurt, Dad, Nana, Papa?

I was led into the sitting room, Mum held me and said, "There's no other way I can break this to you, Papa died this morning'.

The words were like a bombshell. I cried.

'Come and see Nana' Mum said 'She's been very brave'.

I walked to the other room and flung my arms around my Grandmother. Tears fell like raindrops, until all my emotions were drained.

'How?' I asked.

He was just sitting on the bed, getting his breath when he collapsed, and he was probably dead before he fell'.

Dead, dead, dead, dead, the word ran through my mind, Papa is dead.

Memories flashed back, when he used to push me in my small pram when I was young.

His teasing, his twinkling eyes when he laughed.

I cant cry anymore, all I can do is remember, it hurts though.

The words 'Papa died this morning', kept on in my head for days.

I couldn't stop them, it was like a disease, my whole body longed for him to be back. I hoped it was just a nightmare.

I couldn't accept the fact he was gone. I expect I will have to soon though.

I long for the day when I can think about him without it hurting too much.

I'll just put on a brave face, its all I can do.

This is not of course offered as a piece of abstract writing; in the *cognitive* category it is descriptive and interpretative. Nor does the writer raise any moral questions of the kind 'why him?' implying considerations of 'justice'. Rather she is concerned to cope with her own complex emotions. It is the responses in the *affective* category that are most significant.

Nina's grandfather dies, and she feels his loss very deeply. She draws a contrast between the events of a normal day and those after she gets the news of her grandfather's death. She tells of her grief not only through direct expression but also by reporting her words and actions: she is bewildered, is compassionate with her grandmother, and recognises they must live for a time with despair, waiting for the hurt to lessen. It would appear that she has a well-developed understanding of the progress of grief. She shows skill in her selection of action and dialogue to heighten the reader's awareness of the feelings involved. She also shows an understanding of the effect of emotional shock: 'Dead, dead, dead, dead, the word ran through my mind, Papa is dead'; 'memories flashed back'. Here she appears to be going back over the cause of the shock, trying to sort it out, to come to terms with it. Nina compares her experience to a nightmare, even wishing it were so that she could wake up and know that it did not happen in reality. In all she expresses a highly developed sense of the nature of the emotion within herself, an awareness of that of others, and a general disposition to be compassionate, an awareness of the way emotion works in such a situation — the recall of past incidents for example.

The *stylistic* aspect of the writing are interesting. The predominant *organisation* is chronological but interspersed with reflection and flashback. There is a 'prospect' in the first paragraph which gives a 'hint of foreboding'. The last eight paragraphs are essentially reflective. *Cohesion* is less by specific grammatical devices, more by the semantic connection between each section. The use of *syntax* shows control, not only an ability to vary it with the meaning, but the ability to use incomplete grammatical forms for effect ('Dead, dead . . .'; 'His teasing, his twinkling eyes when he laughed').

The most important development to be noted is in the area of lexis, the movement from general unqualified language with little emotional content, to emotionally charged words and phrases, similes, metaphors. There is an attempt to find metaphorical equivalents for the emotion in order to cope with it: 'like a bombshell', 'like raindrops', 'like a disease', 'just a nightmare'. The language may seem conventional, but we must beware of thinking that, necessarily, the emotion is not genuine. Unique expression for unique emotion is a hard-won achievement. In the work of great writers we often find a working through conventional to individual language. Thus poets as diverse as Pope and Blake set themselves an apprenticeship in which they modelled themselves on established writers.

Assessment of argument

The features of the kinds of writing we have looked at above are such as to show up particularly when analysed on the affective and moral models, but less so on the cognitive model. In argumentative writing the reverse is likely to be the case.

The subject, it will be remembered, was 'If children could come to school when they wanted to and could do what they liked would it be a good thing?' The responses of some young children were on the level of assertion. Robert, for instance, is operating on the pleasure principle:

> No school on Friday and Thursday and Tuezday and Monday but Weday come for fut ball.

Slightly less elementary pieces gave a reason for the position taken, as with Dan:

> I think that we ought to be alowed to come school when we like and we wouldnt get so cold in the mornings.

Seven-year-olds are, however, capable of a logical organisation, as in Kate's piece, though this was exceptional in our sample:

I think school should stay like it is. Because if we did not come to school we would not have anafe education to get a job then we would get no money and we would become tramps the we would diey but if we went to school we would get some education and we could go to college then we could get a very good job and get lots of money. So I think school is very good.

She is not restricted to her particular school in arguing her case. She is able to raise a hypothesis in the first sentence, looks first at the consequences of not attending, and finally comes to a conclusion supporting her position. She is able at a certain level to classify and conclude, and we would see her work moving towards the *generalising* class, though obviously at an elementary level.

Kate has dispensed with the narrative line. But it is such a powerful way of organising experiences that children older than Kate hold on to it even when it is inappropriate. Witness Sandra:

To say I would like to do is come to school because of you can learn things out if I did not come to school I think that my mum and dad would say you are going to school if you like or do not like it.

Sometimes I feel like I do not what to come to school to work I just feel like sitting at home but mum and dad said get to school sandra you are not staing at home to day sandra you are getting to school now sandra go on.

I think some times that we are butter at School and that home. Mum says sandra in a way you are much butter being in school. But mum can I just today can I stay home, no sandra, please Just to day no no sandra. When you come home you can go to bed do I have to go to bed yes Sandra.

When I got home I did have to go to bed but I thot that I was best to go to School because I learn more at School and what I will at home like are mum's and dad's can not give us exmahams so . . .

Sandra's is not a logical argument, but fundamentally a piece of description. It is a dialogue, which proceeds by statement and counter-statement between parent and child, a far cry from arguing a point of view. The piece is lively and amusing, and for this reason many teachers would accept it and praise Sandra, whilst perhaps drawing attention to the problems of presentation. To do this would be to have an inadequate 'model of discourse', to think that 'good English' is in some sense one thing. Narrative is not the same as argument, autobiography as explanation, and so on. Differing aspects of competence are required for differing functions. In fact Sandra is avoiding the issue, fundamentally the problem of logical thinking on paper. (For fuller discussion see pp. 41.)

Let us take one further example, a piece from the middle range of 13-year-olds. These writers, like Colin, for example, tended to see something of the complexity of the issues, recognising that there are two parts to the logic — the question of optional attendances and the student choice of activities:

No, there would be so many difficulties inherent in this idea that it would be a non-starter. A few of the problems would be (1) A fluctuating demand for teachers (everyone might come one day and but a few another day). (2) Some children not realizing the importance of education would never come (3) How literally is the above question taken (could children go to school at midnight if the late film isn't any good?) (4) Some children would attend school 4 or 5 hours every day, they would be at a very different level of understanding in the subjects than the people who seldom came and it would therefore be impracticable to put them in the same class, and as only 20 people might want to do RE it would be impractical to split the class into the necessary 4 or 5 levels. (5) In a school of 1600 it would not be possible to let children do exactly what they want (only 4 or 5 people might be interested in falconry). (6) The planning of the curriculum would be a nightmare. (7) The school lunch system would be useless as the lunches might be left one week and over subscribed the next. These seven points show just how ludicrous that sugestion really was.

He starts with an overall evaluation which he proceeds to justify. Each of the listed items is a relevant difficulty, leading to the conclusion. Each item gives a reason for the impracticability concerned. He is at the level of *generalising*. He is beginning to classify, but has not built up a classificatory system — for example by discerning the various issues in the topic and discussing them in turn. He has, however, clearly outgrown the need to organise this type of material chronologically.

The cognitive model has more detailed dimensions which we will not use here, and we have not demonstrated the higher reaches of thinking which was found in a few 13-year-olds. But perhaps enough has been said to illustrate the general thrust of the model and the kinds of insights it gives into children's writing.

Comment

As an introduction to the book, this chapter has summarised the original Crediton Project. It has given examples of how it is possible to describe the written composition of writers of ages seven, ten, and 13 in terms not only of its style but also in terms of its 'psychological content', by which we mean the quality of thinking, the quality of feeling, and the nature of the moral attitude displayed.

To those countless millions who consider that the purpose of setting compositions is to produce errors in spelling, punctuation and grammar, for teachers with little else to do to correct, news of this approach will be greeted with shock and disbelief, and they will read no further. The others, however, the select few who believe that writing develops the human soul, now find themselves at the start of the book.

3 Research into writing

Early work: 1907–64

Until comparatively recently very little research has been carried out into writing in education. This is remarkable when we realise how well the century opened, particularly with the work of two men, one an American, J. M. Rice; and the other an Englishman, P. J. Hartog.

Rice was a pioneer educational research worker. As early as 1903 he made an extensive study which strongly suggested that the training of formal grammar had no beneficial effect on children's written work; and by 1929, when R. L. Lyman brought out his *Summary of Investigations*, it was only possible to assert a beneficial effect through ignorance (or defiance) of the evidence of a large number of empirical studies. Thereafter the research multiplied still more and the results were the same, culminating in a massive study by Maccauley in 1947. Then in 1962 came Harris's thoroughly indecent exhumation and reinternment of the corpse (Harris, 1962; 1965). Admittedly there has been little research since then, but this is merely because there is no point in it. It is after all centuries since anyone took the trouble to demonstrate that the earth moves round the sun. Nevertheless, in over 80 years since Rice's work it has proved quite impossible to get his message across to some teachers, many parents, and most, if not all, politicians. This cannot really be called one of the success stories of the century. The other story, concerned with the work of P. J. Hartog, is moderately less discouraging.

Hartog was a university teacher and administrator. In 1907 he published *The Writing of English*. The opening of Chapter IV sums up the general argument: 'We have seen that the English boy cannot express himself in English, while the French boy is capable of expressing himself in French'. He therefore continues: 'Thus the use of French methods as a remedy for English incompetence, in this matter seems clearly indicated'. It must be said that the evidence for 'English incompetence' is not very convincing. It is the form of highly opinionated quotations from such people as 'a banker', 'a Manchester merchant of standing', the Commander-in-Chief, and the headmaster of Charterhouse who (incredibly for a countryman of Pope or Jane Austen) declared that the English instinct for language was 'more slovenly, more slipshod, and less sensitive that that of any other European people' (Hartog, 1907, p. 4). But the fact that Hartog quotes some comedians does not affect the book as a whole; it must count as a notable piece of research. A sample of schools in Paris was visited on two distinct occasions and other enquiries made. Conclusions were drawn and reported with a specific lesson described, and a piece of written work evaluated. Hartog picks up two things from the French — the training in systematic writing, and the analysis of the classics as models of style — and demonstrates them in specimen lessons from his own teaching. By all accounts he was a good teacher, and the techniques seem far less arid in his hands than in their original French context.

Writing is regarded by Hartog primarily as a means of developing thinking. He speaks of the three aims of writing as being: to enable the writers to record their own observations and thoughts; to explore and elaborate these thoughts, and to develop their own powers of thinking; and to convey to other people the results of their thinking as clearly and completely as possible. Interestingly enough Hartog is somewhat disparaging of the expression of feeling. Contrasting a French boy's description of a fair with what an English boy 'would have' written, Hartog comments of the latter:' Most of his adjectives would have merely suggested his own sensations, and have been utterly useless to a reader trying to form a picture of the fair' (p. 35).

Even so the teacher must always respect the individuality of the child. And this valuing of what the young writer has to say is one of the underlying principles in the eight point summary Hartog gives of the method he advocates:

(1) You find that the average English child of from ten to thirteen can speak easily, forcibly, correctly, *when he wants to say something.* In order to develop his power of speaking and writing easily, forcibly, and correctly, you make him want to say something.

(2) You make him want to say something of his own, something that he feels to be, and that is, worth saying, something on which he has a right to have an opinion. He is not repeating to you what you know already. He is observing external nature and his own sensations and recording his observations, and so doing in a modest way 'original work'.

(3) In writing he is not merely writing vaguely, as our schoolboys at present write essays on lofty themes for the world in general; he is writing for a particular audience and with a particular object in view.

(4) In order to achieve his object he must order his thoughts on a definite plan and present them clearly. The object in view soon makes the schoolboy agree with Pascal and Buffon that orderly thinking is the very basis of style.

(5) His writing stimulates, as nothing else in the school curriculum can do, the imagination of real things (to be sharply distinguished from the

fairy-story imagination); the picturing of consequences that forms the greater part of what we call 'common sense', and that serves as a guide for most of our actions in daily life.

(6) In order to write consistently and with an object strictly kept in view, a continuity of attention is demanded such as is demanded in no other subject but mathematics. And here I would point out that, in the view of M. Payot, who was written invaluable articles on 'Active methods of teaching the mother tongue', continuous exercise of the attention in reality implies supreme exercise of the will. Certainly concentration is one of the hardest lessons for a child to learn.

(7) Besides this power of concentration there is called into play a power hardly exercised at all in school mathematics, a power no less useful in daily life, which one may call, to borrow a term from the science of the oculist *mental accommodation*, the power of changing one's mental focus, of seeing a thing first as a whole, in plan, and then in detail. 'He that cannot contract the sight of his mind' says Bacon, 'as well as disperse and dilate it, wanteth a great faculty'.

And finally (8) — and I regard this as of fundamental importance — you make each child himself the judge of what he has done. He learns to work to satisfy not his teacher but himself. It is the business of the teacher and of the class to make the standard of satisfaction a high one. This is an ideal absolutely opposed to mediaeval ideas. Authority has a place, and a large place, in education; its place has been hitherto, I believe, too large a one in English education for individual efficiency. In this particular work it is the child's own judgement that must be made supreme. His original effort to produce is to be controlled and guided by self-criticism. The aim of the teacher is to cultivate what I will call the *intellectual conscience*.

This, it will be appreciated, is a quite remarkable document, which has by no means been superseded. We may claim to practice the precepts about motivation and having something to say. It is now generally accepted writing 'should be for a particular audience with a particular end in view' but this acceptance did not occur until reinforced by the work of the sociolinguists in the 1960s and 1970s. The responsibility of the individual writer to judge and revise what he has written, exercising 'intellectual conscience' is one we are just beginning to consider with the fashionable 'process' approach. What we have scarcely come to terms with at all is Hartog's emphasis on cognition — its relationship to style, to overall and detailed planning ('mental accommodation'), its development through writing. This point needs to be emphasised. By 'imagination' Hartog does not mean what he rather contemptuously dismisses as 'fairy-story imagination' but the 'picturing of consequences', that is, hypotheco-deductive thinking, in relation to the problems of daily life.

Rice mistrusted grammar from experiment, Hartog from experience, but mainly what they had in common is that they were prophets to whom few listened. Hartog's ideas indeed were being supported in an English Association lecture on the Writing of English delivered in Liverpool in

1908 by J. H. Fowler (Fowler, 1932), and were taken up enthusiastically by the only official report on English before the Second World War, *The Teaching of English in England* (HMSO, 1921). The bare message that English composition should be *taught* has to be seen against a background of English emerging from classics as a subject in its own right, and was progressively accepted. But *how* it should be taught, the detailed insights and observations in Hartog's methods, was not.

The first book specifically on writing after Hartog, Gurrey's, *The Teaching of Written English* (1954) was not a research document. One way in which ideas on writing have been offered in English teaching is through books by scholars and teachers generalising from experience (for example, Stratta *et al.*, 1973; Minovi, 1976; Thornton, 1980; Protherough, 1983; Beard, 1984; Gannon, 1985). Gurrey's was such a book. He reinforced the concepts of audience and function from Hartog, but his main contribution was to emphasise 'motivation' and 'experience', two terms which were part of the essential vocabulary of the creative writing movements of the time. For now we are moving into a different climate. The experience in question is the child's own past experience. It is also current experience which he can be brought into contact with. This was often provided in the classroom. A trainee teacher supervised by the present writer, attempting a controlled conflagration in a baking tin, set the curtains on fire, and the class produced creative writing of quite unusual vivacity.

The creative writing movement was furthered principally by books which might be described as anthologies of examples, usually with commentaries. The most notable of these were Pym (1956), Hourd and Cooper (1959), Ford (1960), Langton (1961), and Clegg (1964). It was of course recognised that there were other forms of writing, named in Clegg as 'recording', but the emphasis was essentially on the children's self-discovery and expression, on their 'coming into their own', 'on self-contained, even self-conscious pieces of writing' (Ford, 1960, p. 1), on the 'very culture of the feelings' (Holbrook, 1961, Chapter 4). Hourd's title, *The Education of the Poetic Spirit* (1949) aptly summed up the programme. There was no doubt amongst its advocates that creative writing also profited other forms of writing, the children 'deriving confidence and fluency from it, and stocking up for recording work when it is called for in history, science and so on' (Thompson, 1964, p. viii). The classification of other forms of writing as 'recording' does not indicate that they were held in very high esteem.

Of the books listed in the previous paragraph, Pym's comes closest to being an empirically-based study. The basic idea was to give the writers a stimulus but as little guidance as possible on the way they should write: 'write in any way you like'. Stimuli were offered ranging from poems, music, opening lines, and pictures, to single objects such as a key, a frying pan, a necklace, a rain hat: sometimes sounds, sometimes smells, sometimes objects to be felt. One of the 'objects felt not seen' was a cucumber (Pym, 1956, p. 79), but unfortunately no results are reported. Attempts were made to classify some of the compositions, but tentatively. The interest was less in analysis, more in the development of fluency, in tapping 'sources, individual, authentic, vital' (p. 11). Evaluation was in fact not highly regarded for this form of writing. A teacher quoted with approval said: 'How can one child's thoughts be better [i.e. worth more marks] than another's?' The answer to that question would not be understood by the person who asked it.

The outstanding theorist was Hourd, whose *Education of the Poetic Spirit* appeared as early as 1949, mediating a literary-critical and a psychoanalytical tradition. Ford (1960) compiled an anthology from national contributions; Langton (1961) from her own pupils' work — she coined the term 'intensive writing', one form of which resulted from line-by-line instructions to the children. Clegg (1964) as a chief education officer was able to gain wide publicity for the writings of West Riding children. Creative writing is still with us and we owe this not a little to the work of such people as these. It certainly stressed the private and individual as against the public and social modes of discourse. But this was necessary at the time, and is still necessary today. But no writer on the subject seems to have advocated the abandonment of writing conventions, even though a piece of research by Heath (1962) suggested that they were better taught through wide reading than by exercises. Pym, for example, is careful to stress that 'free writing' is for occasional use for particular purposes, amongst other modes of writing. It is very doubtful whether the 'progressive' teachers, with their raving disregard for all constraints of custom, were very much more than figments of their critics' imaginings.

The second phase 1964–75

At this point we may describe the state of affairs in the 1960s. Creative writing was well established in the primary schools; a large amount of writing for the purposes of 'recording' went on in the secondary schools, largely determined by the type of work in a variety of subjects required by external examinations. A theoretical basis did exist for the creative writing, as we have seen; but there was no such theory in the other area, the cognitive, nothing for instance of the stature of Hartog's. Nor was there any synthesising concept for the two. In other words a theory of discourse was lacking.

However, influences were converging; concepts such as audience and function from Hartog, as mediated through Gurrey, found a coincidence in the contributions of the sociolinguists, a distinctly British tradition stemming from the great work of Firth. A book by Halliday, Strevens, and McIntosh, *The Linguistic Sciences and Language Teaching* (1964), though concerned with second language teaching, proved influential on first language teaching, particularly with its description of 'register'. In the work of the sociolinguists the most significant concept was that of context of situation. A model constructed by Roman Jakobson (1960) was often quoted.

Jakobson outlined a 'speech event' as being an addresser sending to an addressee a message with a context in a code held in common, through a contact (physical proximity, letter, etc.). So much is elementary. What Jakobson did was to emphasise the importance of each of these six factors in determining a different *function* of language. Thus the 'emotive' function focuses on the addresser in that it normally gives an expression of his attitude towards what he is speaking about; the 'referential' is oriented towards context — what is denoted, the cognitive. And so on. Of course such functions are very general, but Jakobson drew attention to the importance of function *as such*, and refinements resulted from the work of other scholars. As far as writing is concerned the effect was to prompt attempts to classify by function as distinct from by, say, genre (essay, lyric, letter) or the traditional rhetorical categories — exposition, argument, description, narration.

The other great influence was that of Moffett. The word 'seminal' is usually applied to something portentous and incomprehensible by reviewers anxious not to look foolish if the work later reveals meaning. Very few books are truly seminal, but in this field, one of them is Moffett's *Teaching the Universe of Discourse* (1968). It is not portentous, and is clearly written; one of his favourite words is 'sensible'. He sets out a programme which other scholars have followed since:

> The most sensible strategy for determining a proper learning order in English, it seems to me, is to look for the main lines of child development, and to assimilate to them, when fitting, the various formulations that scholars make about language and literature (p. 14).

Moffett regarded growth as predominantly a cognitive matter for which he drew up categories, and saw cognitive developments as having linguistic correlates.

This, then, was the climate in which the Schools Council was constituted to finance research, and it funded the first major UK project to be carried out in this field, the 'Development of Writing Abilities', and the Writing Research Unit was set up at the London Institute. The intention of the project was 'to create a model which would enable us to characterise all mature written utterances and then go on to trace the developmental steps that led to them' (Britton et al., 1975, p. 6). The basic idea in the model was that 'the writing of young children is often very like written down speech', speech with all its tentativeness, loose structure, changes of direction, informality as in conversation or gossip (not of course as in the organised form of 'a public speech'), speech that 'stays close to the speaker' and hence is fully comprehensible to 'one who knows the speaker and shares his context. It is a verbalisation of the speaker's immediate preoccupation and mood of the moment' (p. 82). This the researchers call 'expressive' language, and comment: 'Looked at developmentally [expressive language] seems to be the mode in which young children chiefly write' (p. 11). From this expressive language 'as seedbed' more differentiated forms of language develop. On the one hand we as adults frame the tentative draft of new ideas as expressive: on the other children seem naturally at home in it and seem to move towards other modes through it. These other modes, in writing, are classified on the one hand as 'transactional' and the other as 'poetic'. Transactional language is the language to get things done — to record facts, exchange opinions, construct theories, conduct campaigns (for example — reference books, scientific treatises, political speeches). Poetic language is that used as an art medium, an 'object made out of language'. It exists *'for its own sake*, and not as a means of achieving something else' (p. 91) (for example not only poems, but also plays, novels, songs).

As a model to 'characterise all mature written utterances' this does not get us very far. It is like trying to fit them into one of two boxes and then closing the lid before they jump out again. How does a history book 'get things done'? Why is not Gibbon's *The Decline and Fall of the Roman Empire* an example of the 'poetic', like Waugh's *Decline and Fall*? As an explanation of how these two categories originate — from the expressive — it is equally limited. (The Unit admitted their evidence had not demonstrated this (p. 197). To take just one example, sense of narrative — the basis of the poetic — is strongly developed in pre-school children and seems to proceed directly from speech to writing without the need for an expressive phase.

In tracing the 'developmental steps' leading up to the mature written utterances the Unit makes no suggestions for the poetic but offers a hierarchical description of 'informative' writings as steps in the transactional area. The lowest level is that of 'recording' — 'the speaker describes what is going on here and now' (p. 182), as in 'The policeman's coat is blue with silver buttons'. The next level is 'reporting'. The speaker reports 'what went on or what was to be observed on a particular occasion at a particular place'. The third level is 'generalised narrative or descriptive information': the speaker 'reports what goes on or used to go on habitually' — such as what we do on Sundays. There are seven levels in all, climbing to the 'tautologic' – the systematic combining of abstract propositions leads to new conclusions which form a further extension of the theory or 'system'. Clearly the term 'transactional' is not helpful; we have here the classical Piagetan cognitive categories applied to writing.

Despite its limitations (the researchers had difficulty getting many of the pieces to fit the categories) this is a notable attempt to classify writing, not in terms of literary criticism but of cognitive operations.

The investigation was important less for its research results, which were disappointing, than for the insights into language which it offered. Concepts such as function, sense of audience, spectator/ participant were developed and have become part of the international mentalanguage. A good deal of follow-up activity has been generated at home and overseas. Severely damaging criticisms of aspects of the project's intellectual and methodological procedures were made by Williams (1977) (reply by Britton *et al.*, 1979) and Whitehead (1977), but in all this it has to be remembered that it was the first major project in writing ever undertaken in the UK. And even a restriction of the description of development to the cognitive, whether deliberate or not, could be said to have been a necessary astringent in the climate of the time.

A further large-scale piece of research, the 'Writing Across the Curriculum Project' (1971–5) followed from the Unit (Martin *et al.*, 1976). Interest in language in other subjects of the curriculum besides English had been apparent in the first project, and in the meantime a paper by Martin (1971) gave further publicity to this interest. No evolution of the original model took place, the intention being to make sense of the initial work in the context of a variety of classrooms. Thus findings as such were not presented, rather the detailed incidental wisdoms which arise in an interactive learning situation. Martin followed up the implications of the model in the primary school classroom by studying a week's output of three classes of children aged seven, nine and 11. Teachers, some of whom were members of the project team, produced a book (Burgess, *et al.*, 1973) consisting mainly of examples of children's 'purposes' in writing in a variety of modes, planned on the London model. The concept of language across the curriculum was commended in a slim chapter in the Bullock Report (1975), and work has continued to the present. However, a recent official view as published by a group of Her Majesty's Inspectors (HMI, n.d.) sees the concept as provoking unnecessary territorial challenges to other disciplines, and as regarding as a language problem what is a wider learning problem (pp. 18–20). For whatever reason, it does not seem to have gone as far as was hoped.

The year 1975 has been chosen as the final one covered in this section because it marks the publication of the Bullock Report, which captured the thinking of the 1960's and earlier 1970s, much of it invaluable. However in the mid-1980s our perspectives have changed. To take one example only, the Bullock Report is 609 pages long; of these, seven are devoted to writing.

The situation since 1975.

This chapter is principally concerned with research in the United Kingdom, but there is nowadays a world community of scholarship and it is therefore proper to attempt to sketch in the main trends of its work.

One of the main emphases has been on 'process' — how a 'product' comes to be written and is written. The initiating studies are two, one American, other British — Emig (1971) and Stratta *et al.* (1973). In *The Composing Processes of Twelfth Graders* (1971) Emig describes how she collected information about the previous writing experiences of eight students, and asked them to compose aloud, 'to express orally the thoughts and feelings that came to them while they were engaged in writing three short themes during individual sessions with the investigator' which she tape-recorded. This device limited the choice to articulate subjects who were good writers and inevitably affected spontaneity, but gave the conscious perceptions of the students as to the nature of their problems and tasks. From this data she described the 'dimensions of the composing process' amongst these students as being: the nature of the stimulus; prewriting; planning; starting; composing aloud; reformulation; stopping; contemplation of product; apparent teacher influence on the piece. Emig saw the most promising implications of the study, for the classroom, as possibly ameliorating 'teacher illiteracy' against those many who were without direct experience of the creative process (for instance by writing themselves) and thus insufficiently sensitive to it. On the research side she hoped for further 'characterisation of behaviours involved in composing aloud' (p. 96) on the assumption that 'a writer's effort to externalise his process of composing somehow reflects, if not parallels his actual inner process' (p. 40). This is of course arguable. For instance the act of externalising could change, or even substitute a different strategy for, the original.

In *Patterns of Language* (1973) Stratta, Dixon and Wilkinson described workshops in places as far apart as Winnipeg and Ilorin, in which teachers wrote in response to certain experiences, proceeding through a series of drafts in consultation with a tutor. They were asked to reflect upon this both in terms of their own learning and in terms of its relevance for their pupil's writing. The authors describe the process as being a means of discovery of one's self, a working through of conventional responses in early drafts, arriving at a 'threefold uniqueness' of expression, forms, self: the writers had discovered what they wanted to say, and how they wanted to say it, through the process of doing so.

Since such studies a 'conference/process' movement has developed, the 'conference' being the conferring between pupil and teacher in the writing process. Studies directed by Graves at the University of New

Hampshire have been concerned with the writing process of young children, particularly the first four grades. Such studies focus on the acts of composing by observing and recording (by audio and video) the processes as they happen, and the revisions that are subsequently made. Statistical generalisations are not sought: the case-study method is employed, and the sample is small — a major project supported by the National Institute of Education focussed on 16 children (Graves, 1982; 1983). From descriptive research of this kind it is difficult to draw generalisations. The work establishes the increase of the children's control, and the different strategies of revision they employ and find useful. The researches advocate individual conferences with each child, but are insistent that ultimately the child should retain control. Graves's work has had a considerable influence in Australia through the enthusiasm of the Primary English Teachers' Association and a process diagram offered by Walshe 1982 is well known:

> Prewriting — the experience of a problem, incubating
> Writing — drafting, revising, editing
> Post-writing — publication, reader response, writer's own evaluation.

In the United Kingdom where 'conferencing' is an established part of first school practice there has been much less response. It may be that the gains of the movement arise from the beneficial effects of interaction rather than on success with particular techniques. 'Revision' by children, for instance, does not receive a good press from research (see Purves and Takala, 1982). To take just one example, in examining the revisions of eighth-grade children (what they call the 'compare, diagnose, operate' process), Scardamalia and Bereiter (1983) found the revised versions to be worse as judged by experts, and argued that the children lacked the necessary internal feed-back system.

Another trend is the study of writing development. For many years it was felt that development could be described in terms of countable surface features — quantity and variety of words, phrases, sentences, parts of speech; complexity of sentences, degrees of subordination and so on. The most substantial study on these lines ws carried out by Loban (1963; 1976) who tracked a group of children for 13 years. He started with 338 and at the end 211 were left. Such research is the victim of its own methodology. Its instruments can only make statements of the order that children aged 12 write longer sentences and use more words than children of seven; it can say nothing about meaning. A report by Harpin *et al.* (1973) is (or should be) the final report in this particular tradition. Concerned with writing development in the junior school, it used the following measures: sentence length; clause length; a subordination index; a subordination scale from Loban; use of simple sentences; use of complex sentences; use of 'uncommon' subordinate clauses (all except adverbals of time and noun subjects); the incidence of non-finite constructions in the main clause; general index of personal pronoun use; proportion of first and third person uses; and the proportion of personal pronoun uses other than as subject. Harpin *et al*. find that their results agree with those of other workers only on the value of clause and sentence length, and to some extent on subordination index, as indicators of maturity. From their research it is quite clear that the context of situation is the most important variable. It is to be hoped that this authoritative study will dispose once and for all of a line of enquiry in which language features are not related to context or meaning (see also Harpin, 1976).

A more promising approach is that of the cognitive psychologists. The major problem of the beginning writer is seen by Scardamalia (quoted in Bereiter, 1980, p. 80) as the stupendous number of things which must be dealt with simultaneously in writing — handwriting, spelling punctuation, organisation, clarity, rhythm, euphony, reader reaction and so on; 'To pay conscious attention to all these would overload the information-processing capacity of the most towering intellects'. Bereiter sees successive forms of organisation occurring with increasing automation: associative (relating word to symbol); performative (increasing conformity to convention); communicative (increasing reader awareness); unified (increasing self-evaluation); and epistemic (thinking through writing). Much of the work in this field has once again a strong cognitive concern. However, Kirby and Kantor (1983) have looked at development on an egocentrism–perspectivism continuum. Kroll, Kroll and Wells (1980) use cognitive and stylistic categories with the writings of nine-year-old children.

In strong contrast to the cognitive psychologists, Harrison (1979; 1983) belongs to a distinctly British line of scholarship whose model is literary-critical and psychoanalytical rather than cognitive or linguistic. He is concerned with the stages of the growth adolescent writers: the sample was all the pieces of writing done by a class in English studies during their fourth, fifth and (if they stayed on) sixth years at comprehensive school. Five stages of growth are discerned. It is difficult to do justice to these in summary, particularly since the author is concerned with the complexity and wholeness of experience at each stage. Harrison freely acknowledges the influences of a group of thinkers such as Hourd, Polyanyi and Winnicott in which the values of self-searching as a prime feature in relation to education are emphasised (Harrison, 1979, p. 82). He is not concerned to produce an objective report; rather does he share some of 'a novelist's desire to generate personal recognition in the reader' (Harrison, 1983 p. 1).

Dixon and Stratta (n.d.) study development in narrative based on personal experiences. They have described certain 'staging points'. They draw from a study of texts four questions which 'effectively form a set of criteria' (p. 1):

1   What kinds of ordering or reordering occur as the writer imaginatively recovers the events of the past — and to what effect.
2   Is the writer assuming a reader already acquainted with setting, character, or events?
3   Does the writer remain largely egocentric, or is there a more comprehensive perspective developing in which the thoughts and feelings of other participants are more fully realised?
4   What significant uses of language are there?

From the data the writers posit tentatively four 'staging points' — the first an oral, the final a full literary model, in which the features are perceived as developing in the manner implied by the criterion questions. These criteria are modified in relation to imagined stories (Dixon and Stratta, 1982b) and indeed a characteristic of this work is the recognition that different criteria are applicable to different genres.

Contributions to the study of writing have been made on the whole by educationists and psychologists, and much less by linguists. Kress (1982), a notable exception, points out that the dominant grammatical model from 1965 onwards was that of transformational grammar. By its obsession with the ideal sentence and its contempt for context it was unable to comment on extended context-based discourse such as writing. Kress considers as a measure of growth the development of the concept of 'sentence' in children's writing. He sees speech as punctuated by events and thus argues that 'sentences in early writing are primarily textual units, and that the child's attempt to work towards a definition of a sentence is a textual rather than a syntactic process' (p. 75). The research is novel in that it attempts to apply the instruments of discourse analysis to children's writing.

Comment

The century started well. English was emerging from the classics as a subject in its own right. Rice and Hartog pointed the way forward full of joy and hope. Now their ghosts haunt us, shaking their luminous heads reproachfully.

To Rice we can offer the consolation that, after 80 years, amongst English teachers themselves, the battle is won — no one believes in teaching grammar to improve written composition. But what of others, he will say, with power and influence over education, who loudly proclaim otherwise? And he knows we cannot answer that, for to these people learning of grammar represents a disciplining of the flesh, a punishing of the rebellious spirit, and the ultimate guarantee of a stable society. In its very uselessness lies much of its value.

To the ghost of Hartog we might give a less abject reply. We can say to him that after 50 years his 'not writing on lofty themes for the world in general' but 'for a particular audience with a particular object in view' became the message of the sociolinguists from which were crystallised concepts like function, context, sense of audience. He would be somewhat mollified by this assurance. Even so his main reproach would remain: that the training of the mind which is a principal function of composition has been neglected. Let him speak in the language which the Newbolt Committee used to paraphrase his words (HMSO, 1921, p. 72):

> Composition cannot be regarded mainly as a subject. It is a measure of all that has been truly learnt, and of the habits of mind which have been formed. In fact the capacity for self-expression is essentially the measure of the success or failure of a school, particularly on the intellectual side

We should of course beware of attaching to 'self-expression' here the connotations it later acquired.

We have to agree that this view of writing as a cognitive act has not had the attention it deserves. Certainly there has always been a good deal of low-level cognitive writing — recording, note taking, fact compiling (for one among so many testimonies see (DES 1979, p. 83) — but not enough of the kinds of activity implied in phrases of Hartog's like 'mental accommodation', 'intellectual conscience' or 'the picturing of consequences'. Interest in such activities seems to have waned so much that by 1968, when a high-level team of American educators visited the United Kingdom to review the teaching of English, they found much to praise, but remarked with considerable delicacy: 'Few would maintain that many of the programmes stretched the intellectual powers of the pupils' (Squire and Applebee, 1969, p. 115). But, as we have seen, what we neglected was being developed in the United States. (For a recent wide-ranging view of the research see Purves and Takala, 1982.) We can, however, point to the cognitive ('transactional') scale of the London Writing Research Unit (Britton et al., 1975); to the cognitive model of the Crediton Project outlined in the first chapter of this book; and to some other research which will be referred to in due time. Nevertheless the general picture has been such as to justify Hartog's disapproval.

Where we need not be at all apologetic before Sir Philip's disdain (he was later knighted for his services to education) is in the matter of personal, as distinct from specifically cognitive, development through language, which is generally acknowledged to be the particular British contribution. Shafer, an American able to take an objective view, calls this the 'personal experience model' and sees it as evolving from the 1920s and 1930s in Britain. In the post-war years it was given early currency by Hourd and Bell (1953) ('all learning must partake of the nature of growth'), as well as by Gurrey (1954), mentioned earlier. Then in the 1960s came a great flowering: Holbrook, *English for Maturity* (1961), Creber, *Sense and*

Sensitivity (1964), Wilkinson, *Spoken English* (1965), Whitehead, *The Disappearing Dias* (1966) and Dixon, *Growth through English* (1967). This model found its exemplification in the creative writing movement of the time. It is clear that later generations have gained a wider perception of growth than had Hartog, with his dismissive attitude to 'sensations' and 'the fairy story imagination'.

In this chapter we have not attempted to describe all aspects of research into writing (a fuller account is given in Wilkinson, 1985a) but have concentrated on those which will provide a context for the present study. As we have seen, the Crediton Project attempted to define 'development' in a field where this and similar terms like 'growth' and 'maturity' are common coinage, but which few know how to value. (Holbrook (1961) nowhere makes any attempt to define 'maturity': the nearest we get is a hint that it is the kind of quality possessed by dubious old countrymen who sing saucy ballads.) Thus the Project offered descriptions in terms of cognitive, affective, and moral features as well as of stylistic. The cognitive model pointed in a direction forgotten since Hartog, except by the London Writing Research Unit, and the affective and moral models in a direction the Unit had failed to deal with, that of making some description of growth in these areas.

The present book goes far beyond the earlier study in attempting to relate cognitive, affective, and moral elements to a coherent theory of development; in making certain refinements to the models, particularly the affective; in extending their application to older age groups; and finally in considering their application to the classroom, not only as assessment instruments, but in prompting the kinds of activity that should be going on, that is, providing a model of written discourse.

The last word should be left to Hartog (1907). He has many wise things to say; perhaps what comes through above all is his compassion for the learner. On the right of the pupil to his own opinion he says:

> He will be saying something that he himself has thought out, not telling you what you already know. Your task is to see that he earnestly tries to fulfil his own aim. The guidance that you give, inestimably helped by the public opinion of your class, must be of the gentlest and most tactful kind. It is the training of the growing plant that is your business, not the hammering of a piece of metal with a sledge hammer (p. 60).

4 Thinking and writing

Analytic competence

One of the three aims proposed for the teaching of composition to pupils by Hartog (1907) was 'to stimulate them to explore and elaborate their own thoughts and to develop their own power of thinking'. If this strikes readers of this book as an obvious aim they will be surprised to note that there is no mention of it in the two most significant 'official' documents of advice on English teaching, standing almost a decade apart: the Bullock Report (1975) in the chapter on Writing; and *English from 5 to 16* (DES, 1984, pp. 3, 6, 11). It may be argued that these documents are concerned with the 'functions' of writing. But that is part of the trouble. With function classifications we are concerned with what the writer is doing with writing. There is another way of looking at aims — in terms of what writing is doing with the writer.

Bruner suggests that the constant use of language over and above the mere possession of it makes human beings 'profoundly different' in mental powers; 'and more particularly does it matter that one *writes* and *reads* rather than *talks* and *listens*' (Bruner, 1975, p. 63) because this moves language towards 'context free elaboration': 'The most dramatic step in this direction was the development of notational systems that rendered spoken language into graphic form' (p. 70). 'Linguistic competence' is the possession of the language system, 'communicative competence; is its use in the large variety of social situations. Bruner offers us a third term, 'analytic competence' the development of which is prompted by schooling and particularly by literacy:

> We shall label it *analytic competence*, and its principal feature as with Piaget's formal operations . . . is that it involves the prolonged operation of thought exclusively on linguistic representations, on propositional structures, accompanied by strategies of thought and problem solving appropriate not to direct experience with objects and events, but with ensembles of propositions (p. 72).

'Analytic competence' is fundamental in education. In the last resort the arguments for reading and writing are not in terms of communication, important though this is — one can envisage without difficulty an electronic world in which oral and visual communication are the norm. Ultimately the arguments for reading and writing are in terms of the quality of thinking and feeling they bestow.

This is one of the principles that the present book is concerned to demonstrate, and inevitably a single illustration illuminates only a small part of it. Let us however look at the differences that writing seems to make to a story about a large dog told by an 11-year-old girl (Wilkinson *et al.*, 1974):

The Pyrenean mountain dog (spoken)
this dog that I'm going to tell you about/lives along our lane/he's huge/and it has/long white hair coming over its face/and its face is all squashed/as if someone had pushed it in/this dog's a Pyrenean mountain dog/it's very interesting the way the people who have it now/came to get it/you see/they read in the paper/that/this dog/had killed two alsatians/and the magistrate said it had to be destroyed/and they went up to the magistrate in court/and pleaded for it/and said/we live in the country/and/not many people come out there/so we'd be able to keep it/and so/that's what they did/all the same/this dog still has/still has a reputation/for being fierce/my mother and I once went collecting for charity at their house/and/when we went to the back door/we saw this dog/tied up on a piece of string/and/we never went collecting for charity again there [laughs]/I hadn't/I hadn't seen this dog for quite a time/and so/even though I wouldn't walk past the house/I'd enough courage to go past it on my bike/and one day as I was cycling along the lane/I came round a corner/and there was the Pyrenean mountain dog/even larger than it had ever seemed to me before/and/I didn't know whether to go past it or not/until I noticed that its owner was there/so/I went up to him/on my bike/and I said, 'It won't hurt or bite will it?'/and he said, 'oh no, it's too slow now'/I felt very sad/because/it was so very old/and/often it would keep falling down in front of him/and he'd have to help it up/and pull it up.

The 'Polar Bear' (written)
The 'Polar Bear' is a huge dominating Pyrenean mountain dog. It has a huge, ugly, squashed looking face which is covered by long white hairs. It lives down our lane most unfortunately and has a strange story behind it.

The people who have it now read in the newspapers that this dog had attacked and killed two alsatians, and therefore by order of the magistrate it had to be destroyed. The couple pleaded for it, and were allowed to keep it on the condition they kept it quiet.

However the 'Polar Bear' still has a bad reputation. One day my mother and I were collecting for charity and decided to go to their house. As we walked around the back we saw the dog tied up on what seemed like a piece of string. We never went charity collecting there again.

I had not seen the dog for some time and I could usually pluck up courage to go past their house on my bicycle. One day as I was along the lane I

saw from a distance the 'Polar Bear' and, just as I was about to turn back,
I noticed it had its owner with it. So I cycled on. As I drew near I asked,
"Will it hurt?' 'No dear it's too old and slow.' It was then I noticed how slow
it was, in fact painfully so. I felt then and still do feel very sad because it
seems cruel to keep it alive.

There are obvious differences in the language used in the two versions.
Let us consider some of the differences in thinking which they represent. The written version immediately makes a statement about the
dog, and gives a metaphor to describe it — the Polar Bear. The dog is
characterised by the word 'dominating'. In the spoken version the
behaviour of the dog emerges from the details but there is no attempt
to sum it up in a single term; the nearest we get is that it had 'a reputation for being fierce' but this is one of the specific facts about it. Again,
at the end of the written version a general judgement is made: 'I felt then
and still do feel very sad because it seems cruel to keep it alive.' In the spoken version the sadness is mentioned, but the reason for it is much less
explicit. The writing seems to have given time for the writer to formulate
this view.

The written version is shorter but is in some ways more complete.
Standing back from the court incident the writer is able to give us
the outcome: the couple 'were allowed to keep it on condition that
they kept it quiet', whereas we have to infer this from the court dialogue in the spoken version. Again, partly because it is summary the
written version is better organised in that the essential is being separated out from the less essential. Half way through the written version
is a transitional sentence: 'However the Polar Bear still had a bad
reputation'. This at once refers us back and points us forward to the
further incidents.

Finally we may note the greater exactness of the written version.
The spoken version says the dog is 'slow', the written defines this more
closely: 'I noticed how slow it was, in fact painfully slow.' Again at first
sight the dog seems to have been tied with a piece of string; but on
reflection this seems improbable, and the written version is 'tied up on
what seemed like a piece of string'. We by no means wish to denigrate the
spoken version which is in some way more vivid; the spoken and written
versions are doing different things. The point is that the nature of
the thinking is different. In the written version is demonstrated an ability
to summarise, subordinate, generalise, explain, organise, write exactly, to make a metaphor, which we do not find so marked in the
spoken version.

Similar differences can often be noted between two *written* drafts, but
this only serves to make the point even more strongly that writing is a
means of developing thinking. We shall discuss such differences in the
next section.

Thinking in the writing of seven-year-old children

Let us take the writings of three seven-year-olds considering the problem 'If children could come to school when they wanted to and could do what they wanted to would it be a good thing?' Christopher writes:

> I like to come to school when I like and go home when I like and have ten weeks off school and have one hour at school and have the rest of the day at home.

Kitty writes:

> It wood be stupid if Mr. tomas said go HOME and the bus wannt thire and she had to walk home and her Mum was out and she went to her grans to play with her cat And if we had a choice we whet home and would not learnt anything so we got to go to get a job. Mr. tomar would not have a job.

Kate writes:

> I think school should stay like it is. Because if we did not come to school we would not have anafe education to get a job then we would get no money and we would become tramps the we would diey but if we went to school we would get some education and we could go to college then we could get a very good job and get lots of money. So I think school is very good.

Presumably there would be common agreement about the comparative levels of thinking displayed in each. The first, Christopher's piece, just offers information about his own views. There is no attempt to give reasons or explanations. Doubtless he could give some reasons if asked, but it is normally considered part of thinking to seek and offer explanations.

Kitty also has strong views, but she offers them on the level of interpreting — explaining and deducing (see p. 15). Kitty identifies imaginatively with the situation and thinks about a specific incident in which the children are sent home, and thus speculates what would happen to her. She also gives three general reasons why proposition is unacceptable — children would not learn, would not get employment as a result, and also that there would be consequences for the teacher. The anecdote about the child being sent home is specific and concrete, but two of her reasons (learning, unemployment) are — low-level — generalisations.

In cognitive terms Kate's clearly is the highest level of performance. She begins with a general statement: 'I think school should stay like it is' and the proceeds to justify it. On the one hand come the arguments against not going to school; and then those for going to school. The word 'but' in the third line serves as a pivot for the argument to turn on. Then at the end she sums up her conclusion: 'So I think school is very good'.

Kate's superiority lies in the overall organisation of the piece; everything is linked together, the arguments support the initial generalisation and lead to the conclusion. Not only are relevant arguments included; irrelevant arguments and other matters are excluded. The ability to select in relation to the overall purpose is an important cognitive ability; and the piece is offered on a level of generality. In contrast in Kitty's piece we note a piece of specific narrative (about playing with the cat) which is a mark of young children's characteristic use of narrative as a way of processing experience. And yet if we look at other arguments (school provides an education, which leads to employment) they are very similar to Kate's (Kate is not in fact providing arguments for and against school; she stating positively and negatively the *same* arguments for keeping school). And in fact Kitty provides one argument that Kate does not: that having no school affects other people (such as the teacher) as well as the children.

It seems clear what causes us to think that Kate's composition is at a higher cognitive level is that she has a form for her thinking which we may describe as

Proposition
For
Against
Conclusion

In contrast, judging from what we have here, Kitty has only the narrative form. She tries to resort to it, but it is not suitable for what she wants to do. The question arises: had Kitty used the same form for her ideas would her performance have improved and in that case would her thinking have improved? Or at any rate could we not regard the thinking as likely to do so because the form of her organisation would prompt her to concentrate on certain matters — general points relevant to a particular conclusion, for example?

Perhaps the point of the question can be brought out the more strongly if we ask them about the piece of Sandra's work which we have already seen in another connection.

To say I would like to do is come to school because of you can learn things out if I did not come to school I think that my mum and dad would say you are going to school if you like or do not like it.

Sometimes I feel like I do not what to come to school to work I just feel like sitting at home but mum and dad said get to school sandra you are not staing at home to day sandra you are getting to school now sandra go on.

I think some times that we are butter at School and that home.

Mum says sandra in a way you are much butter being at school.

But mum can I just today can I stay home, no sandra, please Just to day no no sandra. When you come home you can go to bed do I have to go to bed yes Sandra.

When I got home I did have to go to bed but I thot that I was best to go to School because I learn more at School and what I will at home like are mum's and dad's can not give us exmahams so . . .

As one would expect from a ten-year-old, Sandra writes much more than the seven-year-olds whose work we have just looked at. But the narrative form has taken over completely; this is only 'argument' in the sense of a family 'row' (though Sandra knew that such a treatment was not required). What she does is to use a form she feels at home in. No arguments are offered at all until the last paragraph when the single argument for going to school — learning more — is offered. No reasons are offered for the much preferred choice of staying at home except the negative one that her parents cannot give her examinations. In other words, as a cognitive response to the topic given this must rate lower than Kate's and even than Kitty's. And yet it has great qualities, particularly an ear for dialogue and an ability to intersperse it with narrative, which shows on the one hand a capacity to select, and on the other sensitivity to literary models. With such obvious abilities Sandra should have other models to resort to as well as the narrative; models that would not only develop her sense of what is appropriate in terms of styles for particular situations, but would also develop her cognitive abilities.

But of course knowledge of genre is only one of the factors which might contribute to a higher level of cognition. A knowledge of the subject matter, so that the writer knows the relative importance of the elements, is another: yet another is a well-developed sense of readership which could conceivably enable a more accurate choice of words to be made. And so on.

There follows a description of a series of experiments carried out by Kell (1984) to explore some of these matters. Because of their small-scale nature the results are intended as suggestive only.

Experiments on the development of cognition in writing

Five discursive writing tasks were set to each of six eight-year-olds and they were subsequently asked to repeat these tasks after various types of instruction. Thus there were 60 pieces of written work in the sample, from three boys and three girls in a first school. The five tasks, with the modified description used in the school, were

Reporting	Reporting an Event
Instructing	Telling how to do something
Persuading	Giving your point of view
Argument	For and against
Classifying	Organising information

Reporting

In connection with their school sports' day practice the children were asked as 'outside' reporters to make notes and prepare a report in writing which they would be asked to present on video.

The first reports had the features which one would expect: specific details, unjustified assumptions about the audience's knowledge, partial information, lack of overall organisation. A discussion lesson followed which concentrated on two things — the nature of the audience (they were asked to draw them, for example) and thus what they might be expected to know: and the organisation of the report. It was suggested that the event should be introduced, described, and assessed. Perhaps most important, a newspaper account of a school sports' day was shown the children, read out and discussed.

On the whole there were cognitive gains. Sarah, whose first version had been a listing of the three races, gave in her second an introduction which was a summary, followed by a detailed explanation of the skipping relay, concluding with 'and that is woot the First school dud when we went to report of them'.

Michael's first effort was:

> at Woodcroft First School there were three races the relay the skiping and the flat race in one of the skiping races stuart lost the relay you had to go to the person then that person had to run down to the bottom Some people were practising the skiping still peter hibbert was a very fast runner and also a good skiper Ian was with and Ian was cheering Peter in the flat race at the end you run round the hoops.

The piece is introduced well but inconsequently conclude. There is a need felt to explain the relay but this is not done successfully. It is assumed the audience will know Stuart and Ian, though Peter is given an introduction and a surname. On the whole the writing is concerned with specific items, people, and events and is incomplete. The second piece is as follows:

> Woodcroft First School, had a practise for their sportsday in practice the three events were relay, flat race, and skiping. Skipers were still practiceing the flat race had just begon there was a runner that was very fast called peter hibbert he was eight years old there were also sone very good skippers. The running race was good one one of the fastest runners was beaten every body was was saying he beat our fastest runner the relay was very intreasting running up and hands must have ben been ecsastin skiping was very good peter hibbert shot across the field that was unbalieby good and it was a very good day out for reporting

Because of the presentation of this the organisation might escape notice. There is a general introduction, mentioning the three events; followed by an overview of the scene. Then each event is mentioned in turn with some comment meant to interest — the flat race with the excited comments of the crowd, the 'exhausting' relay race, and the 'good' skipping display. The highlight is picked out for the conclusion. The piece has a general viewpoint but can also mention specific details; it is complete; it gives appropriate comment, but leaves out explanations unnecessary in this context. It is clear that the intermediate teaching session has been of great value to Michael.

Instructing

The task chosen was 'How to prepare, make, and fire a clay pot', written for someone who did not know the process but wished to carry it out. The process was familiar to all the writers from their craft lessons.

The first writings on the whole did not grasp what the reader would need to know. Michael is typical:

> First you have to get some clay and some water and then you put it on the table and then you start. first you will have to make it soft then you will have to get the correct shape next you will have to put your thumb in it and then arrange it to make the bottom nice and smooth then take your thumb out. then it need to be put in the clim and after a few days you have pot.

The ambiguities of 'get some clay and water' (without mixing), 'correct shape', 'put your thumb in it' are not realised by the writer. The narrative sequence is of course usable here, but Michael does not know what to assume, and what to state ('put it on the table and then you start' should obviously be assumed).

The best first piece is Wanda's using a chronological sequence classified into stages:

> Telling how to make something.
> Clay making
> 1) First you have to prepare the clay. For this you will have to need it. When you need clay you push the palms of your hand into the clay over and over again. If you find the clay is getting drie then dab a little water on it.
> 2) Next roll the clay in to a ball. When you have got a nice neat ball then press the bottem of it on to your clay board so the bottem is nice and flat.
> 3) When this is done then push your thumb into the ball until you have a hollow in it.
> 4) Next smooth down the sides and tops of the spot with a spatualer. If you think you need some more water then dab a bit on. (You probably will need it).
> 5) Once you've done that then pick your pot up and put it in the kiln. (If there is anything else in the kilm then put it away from them).
> 6) When it comes out of the kilm then glaze it by dipping your pot into the glaze but be careful not to get any on the bottem. Then put it back into the kilm.
> 7) When it comes out again then if you like you can paint it. After you've painted it then glaze it again. Even if you haven't painted it you will still have to glaze your pot.

The discussion lesson concentrated on the children getting the process clear to themselves, for example by drawing the stages; and helping them to envisage the reader — a child who does not know how to carry it out. The writers were given models — instructions for making a toy, and a simple cookery recipe. Again a frame was suggested: Listing materials for the reader — 'you will need'; explaining the process; and conclusion (end product). Wanda's second version is as follows:

Telling How To Do Something.
A Clay pot.

You will need:

A lump of clay.
A clay bord.
Some water.
Spatualer.

How to make:

1) Take your clay and roll it into a neat ball.
2) Then push your thumb into the clay ball and turn your thumb round until you have a nice hollow in the clay. (don't go threw the bottom of the clay ball.)
3) Smooth down the tops and sides of the pot.
4) Your pot will now be fired in the kilm. (before this it will be glazed).
5) When it comes out of the kilm your pot will be glazed again.
6) After this you may paint your pot, and then you will have the finished product.

The listing of materials at the beginning is a gain. In the listing of stages what Wanda has learnt to do is to go for the central points. Unnecessary linkages ('once you've done that you pick your pot up and put it back in the kiln') are excluded. The assumption under item one is now that the reader will know the clay has to be kneaded, and what this means. In the second version the word 'glaze' is used; in the first we were told also how this is carrid out ('by dipping your pot in the glaze'). Both versions have a care to warn the reader what could go wrong, but do it with different details (damping the clay on the one hand, going through the bottom of the pot on the other.)

Here we have something of a paradox. Wanda seems to have made cognitive gains in that she is developing the ability to summarise, and to separate more essential from less essential information; and to produce a more succinct description. On the other hand she has lost the explanation of kneading and the reassurances about the moisture content, which are very good teaching points, made in a friendly informal tone: 'If you think you need some more water then dab a bit on. (You probably will need it)'. She has (temporarily) lost the cognitive virtues of some of her explanations in the first piece. This need not surprise us, nor lead us to think the exercise was not worthwhile. This is one of the features of development, to push forward on one front as against another.

Persuading
The task was to write a letter of persuasion. The head of the corresponding middle school felt it was no longer possible for the first school children to use the swimming pool on his premises. Needless to say this was not the arbitrary decision it appeared to the children; but in writing to him they felt they had a real case to argue. Even the weaker responses have a basis for their argument in terms of 'fairness':

> Dear Mr. Maltby,
> I do not think you should give us swimming lesson because it is not fare for the 1st and 2nd years because They need To get to a good standard like the 4th year.
>
>   Michael

Sally goes a stage further and lectures Mr Maltby with the complete conviction of one confident of divine support:

> Swimming is not dust for you to is for evree one god did not mak it dust for you

Wanda feels that there is no point in not making her feelings explicit:

> If you do not get our point I will think you are really horrid and spiteful

More developed letters point out the consequences of not being able to swim, Peter, for example, hypothising a particular incident in which a child is taken away by the current before the lifeboatman can be summoned.

The discussion lesson followed the pattern already described, focusing on the potential reader, and on a frame for the writing. But in fact the first letters sometimes had features which the second lacked. Thus Ronald's first letter is as follows:

> Dear Mr. Maltby,
> We want our swimming lessons. Its not fair on the little ones they don't know how to swim they might go to a swimming pool and slip and fall in and drown. So if the middle school have all the lessons that could happen so if they can't swim some people might never get there ten metres and 20 40 100 and 200 metres. We should never have them and you should go to dereham pool We realy think that you have had enough and its out turn.

Ronald has three arguments, one in terms of justice, two in terms of the consequences of not being able to swim. He also suggests an alternative as solution. His second letter does not really improve on his first: the text is

> We have got your letter from the about the swimming lessons and we would like are swimming lessons because we raised the money. I think we should go to your pool and you go to the dereham pool. And we held all the bazaars for the money. The first year can't swim and they never will if they don't have swimming lesson

The reasons for learning to swim are not included. One new point is added — that the pool was built from money contributed by fund raising efforts by both schools. This is stated twice.

In cognitive terms, then, there are no gains to be noted. However there is one big gain — the attitude towards the recipient has changed. It is not now felt that the best way to persuade is through abuse of your correspondent.

Argument

The topic was 'Is playtime a good or a bad thing?' The response was one that we observed in the Crediton Project with children of this age (Wilkinson *et al.*, 1980, p. 11), that they failed to notice there were two aspects to the topic, and just argued for one. Thus five out of the six compositions concentrated on the 'bad' side with only one stating both. The 'bad' things were such items as the effects of cold and wet (on the children's legs), accidents (to heads), pushing and shoving, fighting, and lack of positive supervision.

Part of the discussion lesson was lead by Peter with firmness, and several points emerged. The frame offered was

1. Give a personal view on playtime
2. One paragraph for the 'good side'
   One paragraph for the 'bad side'
3. Summary, restatement.

Cognitive gains were all round. Let us take Michael's first version. Although he calls it 'For and against' it is nearly all against. The only virtue he can see in playtime is the negative one that if you refrain from sliding you don't hole your trousers.

> *For and against*
> Play time is a good thing in one way and bad in another way because if you hit someone on the head and hit him back and Mrs. Case is near by its you who gets caught and not the person who hit you in the first place the good thing about play time is if one person is slideing and your not get don't get holes in your trousers because Paul Steed was with me and Danny. Johny pushed Paul off the tyre Paul started fighting then Johnny, got off then Stuart Lomax started fighting with him then luckaly mrs. seaman came alogne and stopped it.

Michael's piece, after listing some of the disadvantages of playtime, goes off into an anecdote about a fight which was mercifully stopped by the teacher. There is one explanation, about how one may be reprimanded for someone else's misdemeanour. Michael's second piece is as follows:

> *Is playtime a good or a bad thing*
> This writing is about playtime.
>   The good side of playtime is you get freash air and meet some of your friends if they are in anouther class and to have nice games and not to fight with each of you.

> Some bad things about play is do not thump each uther unless you want to get told off by the teacher who is on duty. anouther bad thing is that some people just go berserk and have a game of cross cars and some gets heurt by acendent and then that person goes and tells when he did not mean it. then that gets stopped and then some one starts a game of piggy backs then the bell goes then it's all over.
>
> I hope you agree with one of these things, I mean the god are the bad

He starts with a general description of his piece. Then he lists three advantages of playtime — fresh air, meeting friends from other classes, having friendly games. The disadvantages are that you cannot 'thump each other' with impunity and that you might get hurt in a vigorous game by accident. There is a hint of an anecdote, finishing with the bell, but it is by no means so prominent as in the first version. Michael is learning to control his material.

Classifying

The children were asked to write the sale particulars of houses they lived in. The immediate response was to present random information, as we see in the following extracts from Peter:

> We have got a green door and a green garage door. I have got stons on my drive.

and Sally:

> I have 14 stri (stairs). I have sentral heting and a good cooker and lots of kuberds too. We have two pull down lap sadse (lampshades).

Ronald however thinks in general categories:

> The House has 3 bedrooms, 2 toilets, front room, kitchen, dining rom, pateo, and a utility room. The house can take ten people . . . its got central heating radeators in every room.

In his second piece he opens with the same sort of survey and then goes on to describe individual rooms, and so on, in more detail:

> The entrance hall goes off to the lounge kitchen and dining room its not big enough for furniture

All children have difficulty with this task, the absence of an obvious narrative or chronological pattern made the selection of material a problem. Despite guidance about classification in the discussion lesson, and the examination of some house agents' particulars, the children were still in trouble. And yet in principle this level of classification should not be beyond them. It is probable that they were overwhelmed by a large amount of new information in addition to the classifying task. They had difficulty with some of the vocabulary, not immediately understanding for instance terms like 'detached', 'semi-detached', and 'terraced house'.

Comment

Kell (1984, p. 110) summarising the results of the above small-scale experiment, finds the most noticeable developments are a greater sense of form, a reduction in quantity, more ordered classification, and an awareness of the reader. No one would expect a dramatic development in ability to handle various types of discursive writing, but even the small progress observed in some of the experiments, though it may not be long term, suggests that this development may be prompted by teaching. This teaching is aimed primarily at making cognitive gains.

A point made at the beginning of this chapter — about a relationship between form and thought — has been sustained by this data; that there is a relationship between thought and form — that certain stylistic requirements call forth certain types of thinking. Thus even with a simple pro-con frame there was improvement in 'argument' compared with that brought forth by an 'expressive' type of organisation. Another indication seems to be that more exact use of language (and hence thinking) is prompted by focusing on the reader's needs.

It is important to bring out the need for the direct teaching of thinking and discursive writing because it does not commonly receive much attention. The creative writing movement contributed much of value, but it denigrated by implication other forms of language (classing them under the disparaging term 'recording' — see p. 26 above). And in 1975 the term 'expressive' was offered (Britton *et al.*, 1975) and became popular as describing the 'seed bed' of language from which more differentiated forms grew. In this, over-facile analogies were made between the spoken and written languages. It is not to be denied that we find embryonic differentiations in the 'expressive'; the difficulty is that, by naming a whole host of aspects of language as one thing in this way, we make it into a 'stage' through which all must pass with a certain deliberate inevitability. As far as discursive writing is concerned, evidence such as the above suggests that we need not be fatalistic about it and the thinking associated with it. As far as narrative is concerned, there is even a case to be argued that *narrative* itself is the seed bed out of which certain flowers in the 'expressive' garden come, in that narrative seems to be the easiest and earliest *extended* form of speech and writing that children grasp. We have noticed in the above experiments how children reverted to it; how they are bewildered when deprived of its support in the classifying task.

Research on thinking in the writing of adolescents

The study of thinking in the writing of adolescent writers has gone a little further than in the writings of young children, but not much. The pioneering work of Peel (1956), which led him to conclude that 'The late adolescent's thinking flowers into evaluative, critical, penetrating writing' (p. 185), was not followed up specifically in his later work on *The Nature of Adolescent Judgment* (1971), though the books remain highly provocative of ideas. Apart from the Crediton Project and subsequent associated studies (for example, Sternglass, Wittstein), an overseas scholar, Vigar (1985), surveying the literature, finds only few recent studies of note: Dixon and Stratta (1982a), Freedman and Pringle (1984), and Biggs (forthcoming).

Sternglass (1981) considers the Crediton cognitive model as an instrument for diagnosing the levels of thinking of college freshmen. Two essays were give to 200 students after which they were asked to write, the task being defined as 'to elicit analysis of the two essays and to elicit a synthesis of the material analysed' (p. 271). The essays were concerned with the nature of success and failure, and the students were asked to write on 'Views of themselves. Winners or Losers'. Sternglass on the results of the experiment concluded that the Crediton cognitive model proved a useful instrument for classifying levels of cognitive development, particularly since it went beyond making judgements on a narrow range of highly visible features or 'sentence level characteristics' (spelling, punctuation, concord, and so on (p. 274). A good range of discrimination was obtained between descriptive/interpretative thinking on the one hand, and generalising/speculating on the other.

A further study of Sternglass (1985) based on students drawn from three American universities gave three tasks to a cross-section from each. The tasks were explanatory, argumentative and speculative. The explanatory was as described in the previous experiment; the argumentative was a discussion of the reasons for and against attending college; and the speculative was on the characteristics of the family in the year 2000. The study finds the Crediton cognitive instrument as relevant an instrument in describing the writings of the late adolescents in the sample as it was with the original 7–13 age range. An interesting feature of the study is the chapter entitled 'Designing writing tasks to foster cognitive growth', where the writer examines the preconditions for such growth, and suggests, with examples, that the general movement from tasks that call for expository response to argumentative response to speculative response will provide a framework within which increasingly complex cognitive strategies can be fostered.

Wittstein (1983) applies the cognitive, affective and stylistic models to selected writings of four inner-city high-school students, and their relevance to the writings of older adolescents is again confirmed. Her research brings out the need for a cognitive model to underlie the planning of composition courses at college level. She emphasises that the Crediton model, because it is multi-dimensional, 'reminds us that our assignments should not only be cognitively challenging but emotionally satisfying as well. It also reminds us that the writer, like the process we ask him to grapple with, is not linear'. (p. 197).

Both these writers consider the teaching of cognitive modes in the context of the American freshman. Dixon and Stratta concern themselves with argument in the contexts of secondary examining and teaching in the United Kingdom. They argue that a closer definition of functions of argument is necessary. They distinguish the *ruminative or reflective* essay, where the writer may mull over the arguments without needing to formulate a final position; *advocacy*, where the writer recommends or persuades; *arguing through* — presenting conflicting viewpoints and coming to a decision; *attempting an overview*, where the writer represents the range of argument on all sides. The distinction between these categories is not of course absolute, and it is important to stress that they are not hierarchical – to be done well all of them would require the high-level cognitive skills described by Crediton. For example, a barrister presenting a case for the defence is not, in his thinking, only aware of the case for the defence. He has had to carry out an overview of all the evidence, and to speculate on alternative interpretations of it, even though in the end he chooses only to emphasise certain aspects.

It is clear that adolescent writers experience great difficulty with the cognitive writing tasks they are set. This has doubtless something to do with the way they are presented; with their unfamiliarity; with the way teachers themselves shy away from them, in both setting and marking; with low motivation. Biggs (1984) makes a broad distinction between knowledge telling and reflective writing, one being 'linear' the other 'cyclic' in organisation. So often it is the school practice to encourage and reward 'knowledge telling'. Some of these problems are discussed in a stimulating paper by Freedman and Pringle (1984).

They point out that, whereas to succeed in a story the writer has to realise the conventional schema from the genre, in argument there is no such conventional schema. They remind us of the tradition of the rhetorical theory pre-dating Aristotle, which they draw on to define some features essential to argumentation:

> First, the whole piece of discourse must be unified by either an implicit or (more commonly) an explicitly stated single restricted thesis; that is, the whole must be so unified that each point and each illustration directly substantiates the thesis or is a link in a chain of reasoning which supports that thesis. Secondly, the individual points and illustrations must be integrated within a hierarchic structure so that each proposition is logically linked not only to the preceeding and succeeding propositions but also to the central thesis and indeed to every proposition within the text (p. 74).

This relating of narrative to argumentative structure and definition of the latter is most helpful and should prove susceptible of development.

The organisation of experience

We are all the time organising our experience by means of language. In the very act of naming things the young child selects them out from other things and makes possible their arrangement in relation to one another. We organise by classifying – items on our shopping list are likely to be groceries rather than types of gorilla. We organise by associating — for example, people with places (often failing to recognise them elsewhere).

There are, however, two ways of organising experience which underlie these, which depend on two facts about us as human beings. One fact is that we live in a world of time. The other is that we are capable of reason. From the first we learn that events succeed one another relentlessly. If we wish to see one in relation to another then we describe them in chronological sequence; this is the basis of a narrative. From the second we are prompted to see that one thing does not just follow another; it may be caused by it. This is the basis of argument. The temporal nature of life prompts stories; its causal nature prompts deductions.

When children come to organise their experience in writing they are strongly drawn to a chronological presentation, which soon develops into narrative. This is comparatively easy, partly because it can be drawn from observation — people acting in time. For this reason it is often used by young writers where another form would be appropriate — a form based on reasoning. Such forms, which we may signify under the general term 'argument', are much harder to acquire and operate because the events they describe are not apparently happening in the street outside, but are abstractions in the head: questions like 'should we abolish schools?' are not ones which can be decided by writing a school story.

In the earlier part of this chapter we examined the writings of young children. Let us now look at thinking in the writing of further education students, and try to discover how successful it is.

Two arguments compared
A group of students was asked (Vigar, 1985) to write on the proposition: 'For a year after leaving school all young people should be engaged in social work of some sort or other'. Susan wrote:

> When a youngster leaves school it is fundamentally their choice whether they engage in social work. Many youngsters have one aim when leaving school and that is to receive their first pay packet. A fair percentage of social work is usually voluntary and therefore this would be a discouragement to the youngsters.
>   It is perhaps ideal in theory that it would benefit society but difficult to carry through in reality. Many youngsters when leaving school may either feel like taking a year off, or beginning on the paths of their careers. Therefore social work does not fit into their careers.

If a youngsters wanted to enter a career where the social aspect were very important then he or she may well benefit in spending a year in this way. Perhaps it would be better idea to participate in social work as a hobby. For example, a youngster at school or perhaps unemployed would be willing to spend some of their spare time serving the community. If nothing more, it may well impress a future employer as well as giving themselves a feeling of achievement.

I personally feel that many youngsters leaving school could not afford to take a year and spend it doing social work unless it is going to be beneficial to them in their future career. It is therefore totally up to the individual how they spend their time.

Not a very inspiring title.

There is no attempt at definition; the writing begins by stating straight away the line of argument — that the individuals should have choice; and that the choice should be career-orientated. The points are repeated in other words in paragraph two; and summed up in paragraph four. Paragraph three is about the need for career orientation. The final paragraph is a conclusion, repeating the two main points. The argument is not developed though one or two supporting subsidiary points occur on the way through, such as at the end of paragraph three. The phrase 'If nothing more' seems to indicate an afterthought: 'If nothing more, it may impress a future employer as well as giving themselves a feeling of achievement.' There is coherence in the whole, but this is only because no risks are taken; the writer remains with her two points and repeats them. Fundamentally what we have here is 'knowledge telling', in the form of a series of assertions (in the Crediton categories this would be describing, with low-level interpretation (see p. 133)). Only one side of the case is presented; the viewpoint is egocentrical.

In contrast, the work of a more mature writer is marked by the ability to take an overview, to suspend judgement till the arguments are considered on both sides of the case, to relate personal to social considerations. Here are the first paragraphs in the composition by Eileen:

The proposal sounds most laudable in theory, *but* one can foresee enormous problems in enforcing such a project. It can be argued that, with unemployment levels being so high amongst school-leavers, any worthwhile project which will keep them occupied, and by implication, disciplined, can only be to the advantage of the young people and of society as a whole. Much the same argument has been put forward in the argument for re-introducing National Service, but this is male-orientated and these days smacks of unfashionable militarism; a social work programme, on the other hand, could embrace young people of both sexes and all backgrounds. No-one could plead exemption on the grounds of conscience and it could be made a necessary preliminary to, say, university enrolment.

The idea that school-leavers should take a year out before going on to higher education is by no means a new one, and many young people take the opportunity to travel or taste the world of work. To restrict this year to doing social work rather than, say, lumberjacking in Canada, seems to take a narrow view of what constitutes the development of a social conscience. In all probability, a programme of obligatory social work would benefit certain sections of a community, but I suspect it would be very difficult to oblige young adults to do it and it would also prove very costly in adminstrative expenses. The young people would require close supervision which would probably involve too many man hours, and the financial burden on the state and the taxpayer would hardly decrease.

In the first paragraph the general position is reviewed — the proposal would benefit society as a whole. There is a reference outside the immediate problem to the case some years ago of compulsory National Service for men, which serves to indicate how the present scheme would be an improvement. The second paragraph develops main points from the first. Once again the proposal is put in context ('it is by no means a new idea') but it is also evaluated in terms of its moral content: 'To restrict this year to doing work rather than, say, lumberjacking in Canada, seems to take a narrow view of what constitutes the development of a social conscience.' The difficulties, anyway, of implementing it are also foreseen: '. . . I suspect it would be very difficult to oblige young adults to do it but it would also prove very costly in administrative expenses. The young people would require close supervision which would probably involve too many man hours' and the cost to society is recognised, 'and the financial burden on the state and the taxpayer would hardly decrease'. This comparison brings out very clearly one of the features of cognition. It is not just a matter of operating certain mental processes — explaining, generalising, and so on, it is doing this in a background of knowledge — one's 'premises' have to be correct. At an elementary level this means having one's facts right. If a reader of this book is a teapot then she may argue with perfect logic that she need not buy another teapot to entertain guests to afternoon tea. There is nothing at all wrong with the argument, but with the basic premise – that she is a teapot, which is intrinsically unlikely.

At a higher level of thinking the knowledge brought to bear will provide a context, historical, political or social, perhaps — the reference to National Service, and the knowledge of previous experience of the year out. It may enable the writer to comment on motive. In the first paragraph, for example, it gives frame of reference which enables the writer to go beyond the surface intentions of government work schemes in referring to 'any worthwhile project which will keep them occupied, and, by implication, disciplined'.

Other features of more developed cognition which this writing illustrates are the search for definitions and the ability to analyse. The opening sentence tells us that the proposition must be examined closely: 'The proposal sounds very laudable in theory, but . . .' And in the second paragraph, as we have seen, a closer definition of 'the development of a social conscience' is asked for. The quality of the analysis comes out particularly if we compare later parts of this composition with Susan's. Susan, it will be remembered, could not cope with the complexities of the problem, and thus had to reject the whole scheme. Eileen, however, is positive and looks for the conditions in which it might be of use, and the classes of student to which it might be of use.

An optional year, then, could appeal to:

1. young people who are unable to find jobs;
2. those who are unable to decide on their choice of career;
3. those who, for whatever reason, want to take a year out before going on to do anything else.

It would seem likely that the very task of writing is *causing* this student to think clearly on this issue, not only in the details but in overall plan — in general she adopts a pro-con construction.

The students carried out the assignment in class without preliminary planning, so what we are seeing is a working through of ideas at the same time as they are being written. In Eileen's writing this appears in the way she keeps returning to her own experiences as a means of testing the validity of what she is arguing, and in the constant weighing-up of the pros and cons. Even in the paragraph in which she rehearses the arguments in favour of the scheme, she inserts a qualifying note:

> . . . the fostering of a social conscience is no bad thing, but it is a shame that it should have to be obligatory.

By the end of the composition she has argued through to a conclusion in which the complexities are weighed:

> It is very difficult to argue in favour of this proposal. While it sounds as though it would benefit both the individual and society the administration of the scheme would be very difficult, labour-intensive and expensive. It might develop the social awareness of the minority, but on the whole I think any *obligatory* plan would meet with resentment and avoidance. Much better to introduce a voluntary scheme.

Had this essay gone on through further drafts it might have been that some parts would have been subordinated and others rearranged and developed. Thus the matter of 'social conscience' which is mentioned three times in passing might have been made into a main theme — we cannot say. Nor presumably could the writer — the discovery could perhaps only have been made in the discovering. But ultimately the reader is concerned with what is there, not what might have been.

The thinking of these writers is clearly differentiated — the first is stating, describing, asserting, explaining a little; the second is classifying, generalising, speculating on what would be the most desirable outcome, at quite high level (these operations can be described in detail on the original Crediton model). What the comparison between them brings out clearly, as we have observed, is the importance of that other element in thinking, over and above the processes, the frame of reference. Ultimately it is this which distinguishes thinking which is sensible from that which is silly, sane from insane.

Argument as genre

Let us now turn to the matter raised by Freedman and Pringle (1984, p. 79) about the lack of a model, a 'genre scheme' as they call it, for argument. They point out that there is no early training ground for written argument, unlike narrative; and oral argument, being like a tennis match, offers no pattern for individual extended written discourse. These things are true. And yet we do find in everyday language some concepts of the nature of argument which are not applicable only to the spoken language. We refer to the 'line' of an argument ('I want to argue along the following lines'. 'What line are you taking?'). Along these lines are 'points' ('he made several points') which it is necessary to 'stick to' ('don't go wandering off the point', 'don't go off at a tangent') and to understand ('you're missing my point'). Points must be 'supported', 'developed', 'elaborated'. More than this there must be general coherence; the arguments must 'hang together' and be 'weighed', which implies that 'there are two sides to every question'. Not only that but we follow logical steps, and do not go 'jumping to conclusions'.

Popular wisdom does, then, give us guidance about the nature of argument — the taking of a line, the making of points, the need for supporting argument, the need to be relevant, to follow logical steps, to see both sides of the question, not to anticipate conclusions. In particular, in phrases like seeing 'two sides to every question', it gives us what must, by definition, be the key feature of argument, or to put it another way the basic pattern of the genre. The use of these phrases does indicate some general level of understanding of the nature of argument. This is a start, but it is not sufficient, for ultimately the difficulty in writing argument lies in the need to abstract and conceptualise which it demands. Freedman and Pringle (1984, p. 81) are nevertheless hopeful, at least for teachers who are patient, and encourage the reading of allied material, and for writers who are motivated. These are important factors; far too often 'argument' has been required cold, in examinations or other formal situation, away from any context or supporting resources. (We saw with Eileen that ability to supply context improved the quality of her thinking.) Writing argument is difficult because thinking is difficult; but clearly both are essential.

Comment

In this chapter we have argued that writing confers a special quality on thinking. Experiments suggest that younger learners can be helped to think through writing, more than has been believed; and this is certainly true of the older learners. It is often said since Hardy (1968) (see p. 99 below) that narrative is 'a primary act of mind' in that the world is temporal. But argument is also a primary act of mind in so far as the world is logical. It is this which makes thinking through writing so important.

5 The quality of feeling

The education of the emotions

In everyday language we may speak of people being guided by the head or by the heart. An old expression, 'don't let your heart rule your head', means 'don't let your feelings overwhelm your judgement'. The idea behind this, of course, is that we are made up of a 'cognitive' part (head) and an 'affective' part (heart) and that sometimes these are pulling in different directions, the one running away with the other like a pony in a Western. We also sometimes use the word 'emotion' interchangeably with 'feeling', speaking of an 'emotional judgement', or 'letting one's emotions take control'. Sometimes this interchangeable use makes little difference; however in the present discussion a distinction is necessary. It is one given currency by Peters (Hurst and Peters, 1970).

Let us consider 'emotions' such as anger, jealousy, fear, admiration. These do not arise spontaneously, but have an external cause. A person is angry *about* something, jealous *of* someone, and so on. But it is not the cause itself which gives rise to the emotion, it is the judgement the person makes about it and the value he puts upon that judgement — the *appraisal* he gives it. Thus Tom's girlfriend talking sinuously to Dick occasions jealousy in Tom because he appraises the situation as threatening her preference for him, and is *disturbed* by this. Harry, seeing the same conversation, is indifferent to it and makes no appraisal of it. In Tom's jealousy there are two elements — a cognitive element (the appraisal) and a feeling element (the disturbance). Feeling is often spoken of as 'coming over us', as something which often happens to us when we make an appraisal, something which *affects* us — we speak of being 'affected by grief', or being 'seized with passion', and the implication is that we are passive in the matter. For this reason the realm of feelings (and emotions) is sometimes known as 'the affect' or 'the affective'.

An emotion may be described, therefore, as a cognitive act together with the feeling this causes. Peters (Hurst and Peters, 1970, p. 49–50) distinguishes between a cognitive act which he calls a judgement, for example, that something is three feet high, and one which he calls an appraisal. which has a feeling side to it, for example, that something is dangerous:

> That is why the cognitive core of the emotion is referred to as an appraisal and not just as a judgement. But the feeling is inseparable from the cognition; we could not identify such feelings without reference to the understanding of the situations which evoked them.

It is important to emphasise this 'cognitive core' to the emotions as sometimes 'head' and 'heart' are spoken of as though they were completely separate. The appraisal made may be an extremely rapid one. We may take an instant dislike to someone on the basis of a rough exterior, for instance: this appraisal may turn out to have been mistaken when we find out that underneath it beats a heart of gold. But in both cases the feeling of dislike or of liking were based on an appraisal, in one case superficial. Appraisal is frequently an unconscious matter: for instance, we may dislike someone who reminds us of a past enemy. though we are not aware of the reason for this reaction. This kind of reaction is sometimes called 'intuition'; nevertheless it still contains an appraisal.

There follow from regarding 'emotion' in this way two very important implications. One is that we cannot talk of emotional development as separate from cognitive development. The (emotional) response will always be related to the (cognitive) appraisal. A young child might evaluate a teacher as 'cross' or 'bossy'; an adult appraisal of the teacher could be much more complex, seeing for instance such characteristics as functions of role as much as personality. And this brings us to the second important implication: we cannot separate emotional from social development because emotional development takes place predominantly in relation to other people. An emotion of compassion, for example, requires some bing outside oneself to call it forth; so a child may try to console a companion who has fallen. As Peters (Hurst and Peters, 1970, p. 50) says:

> Emotions such as jealousy, guilt, pity and envy cannot be characterised without reference to moral and social concepts such as rules, ownership, and rights. One of the main features of emotional development is the learning of the countless different ways of appraising other people and ourselves in terms of a conceptual scheme which is predominantly social in character. The education of the emotions consists largely in the development of appraisals of the sort which are appropriate in terms of moral and aesthetic criteria and which are founded on realistic beliefs about how we are placed.

To complete this section we may consider two other aspects of appraisal not accompanied by feeling. First of these is the appraisal which, on any particular occasion, does not result in associated feeling. For instance, we may be jealous of someone without 'getting worked up' about it; our jealousy may come out in disparaging remarks we make about him. Here we are more likely to talk of a *motive* of jealousy rather than an *emotion*, a motive being a reason for doing something, in this case making the remarks. Second, there is the appraisal which is associated neither with feeling nor motive for action. This is when the appraisal is made, and the speakers talk *as if* as they were feeling the emotion; 'I'm very angry with Class 3B' their teacher tells them without even a slight rise in blood pressure. 'I'm sorry you can't come' we say to the apologising guest. This sort of appraisal is equivalent to those so frequently used by a practising writer, say a novelist, in the creation of character.

It is difficult to see how *feeling*, in the sense used above, could be educated. It would be like trying to educate the weather — a succession of changes and disturbances — storms, calms, whirlwinds. All we could do would be to let it run its course whilst trying to minimise any possible damage. We do not encourage even young children to behave like that. As soon as they can understand, well before they begin to speak, we begin to influence their cognition, for instance by using terms of approval and disapproval in context.

One part of the educational task is the 'development of appropriate appraisals'. Thus we teach that others should be appraised as requiring friendliness not aggression; so that a little girl is not encouraged to pull her brother's hair, or belabour him with a toy computer. We further try to encourage 'self-transcending' emotions such as sympathy and compassion, and thus discourage childish self-centred behaviour.

The second part of the education task is the canalisation of the affect, which is directed into positive creative activities, not negative destruction ones. A successful American project to rehabilitate vandals uses their aggression to break in wild mustangs. But parents and schools are engaged all the time in furthering similar processes in less dramatic circumstances. One of the features of writing which emerged from our studies is its importance as a way of giving positive outcome to emotions which might otherwise be very difficult to cope with. Of course writing is not the only way. The central fact to bear in mind is that we, as human beings, are creative, and that to create a good move in football, or to contribute a victory or a good defeat at hockey, or to solve a problem in mathematics, is as of much value as a performance in the so-called 'creative arts', the value of which as saviours of the human race are greatly overrated by their advocates.

The language of the emotions

Dunlop, in his excellent book, *The Education of Emotion and Feeling* (1984) makes an interesting observation: 'it might be said that most of the aims of the education of the emotions could be summed up under the heading 'teaching the languages of feeling' providing we interpret the word language in a broad sense.' Language, he argues, fixes what was fleeting, dim and vague. Experience is hard to retain and identify unless it is captured in concepts or some other 'fixed' medium. To 'manage' it we must have some way of distinguishing aspects of it. This argument, which Dunlop uses here for language in general, is one we consider has particular importance for the written language. In his discussion of the 'languages of feeling' he specifically mentions the written language, seeing part of the education of the emotions as to encourage written accounts of emotion, for only then can a precise 'fixing' be attempted. Literature provides us with examples of how this is done.

Dunlop see the language of feeling as being made up of a specific emotional vocabulary; an extension of this is metaphor, poetic language; the use of proverbs, myths, stories, and so on, as vehicles of shared feeling within a culture; and the whole body of language — one's first language contains an immense range of ways of feeling inseparable from the culture; if one speaks a second and further language one is less likely to have access to these in such languages.

We do, however, have to be careful in using terms like the 'language of the emotions', 'the language of feeling', as though we could distinguish these from, say, 'the language of thinking' in any simple way. At first sight some words seem to have a high emotional charge, particularly words connected with power and sex and drugs — 'tyrant', 'fascist pig', 'chauvinist', 'love'; and some do seem to have specifically intellectual meanings, particularly those from academic disciplines — 'triangle', 'sodium bisulphate', 'syllogism'. But, such words as these apart, what most determines the connotations of a word or group of words is the context. 'There will be rain tonight' seems a very ordinary expression, used with very slight variations, on countless occasions by countless people. It is only when we remember it occurs in *Macbeth*, where Banquo says it to his son just before the murderer leaps out crying 'Let it come down', that it becomes more meaningful, the rain symbolising the whole tragedy that overwhelms Banquo.

This is why the original Crediton work on the development of the affect did not look for specific forms of language as evidence, but instead at certain situations in which development would manifest itself. These situations always assumed the self; the self in relation to the self; in relation to others; in relation to the environment; and in relation to the facts of the human condition.

A theory of development

We have seen, then, that affective behaviour cannot concern feeling alone. It has to have a cognitive component. And because we necessarily live in a culture which has certain values, it has a moral component also. A formulation of 'development' was made in the original Crediton Project (see p. 14 above) which seemed to have a certain common-sense validity, but lacked a powerful synthesising concept. For this we need to turn to the tradition of Freud, particularly Erikson as mediated through Jones (1968).

Erikson postulates *nuclear growth crises,* associated with life stages, through which the individual passes. First, there are the nuclear growth crises of trust and mistrust. Infants learn that, to the extent that experience is coherent and predictable, life is basically trustworthy; to the extent that the sequences do not hold together they learn that life is basically untrustworthy. Second, there are the crises of autonomy and shame and doubt. Experience of controlling and being controlled give expectations that they are autonomous: if these experiences are too powerful infants begin to doubt this and feel shame. Third come initiative and guilt. Infants develop expectations that they can choose and act; but indecision and disfavour from others give expectations of guilt. Fourth — now moving from infancy into childhood — we have industry and inferiority. Industry involves learning 'how to', and involves on the one hand acquiring practical skills, and on the other hand adapting socially; conversely failure, hence inferiority, occurs.

The fifth nuclear growth crisis, identity and identity diffusion, is the adolescent one. Identity is disrupted in early adolescence, and is gradually reintegrated through the period, involving a process of emancipation from parents, the striving to be oneself. The sixth crisis, intimacy and isolation, involves sharing with and being shared by another person, and this is intimacy. To the extent that the person learns there are sides of the self that can never be shared, there is isolation. The striving is to share oneself. This would be young adulthood. Adulthood follows and here the nuclear growth crisis is generativity and self-absorption. By generativity is meant a concern with progeny. As Jones (1968, p. 148) writes:

> Thus all humans who reach adulthood experience a very palpable shifting of interest from self to progeny, if only by default. In this sense, we may say that the adult is moved to take special interest in children — his own, those of others, and his brain children — be these theories, paintings, books, bridges, crops, engines, or customers.

The human being is essentially creative: self-absorption is inherently wrong, not because it is morally wrong but because it is developmentally wrong. An alternative word Erikson uses for this is 'stagnation'. Teaching and similar professions are 'generative' because they cultivate growth, and, as Jones says: 'The social modalities specific to adulthood are the modalities of service: to make, to let be, to cultivate growth' (p. 148). To conclude the cycle, Erikson's final stage is old age, marked by integrity and despair, the wisdom to face having been, and not being, 'responding

to the need of the on-coming generation for an integrated heritage'
(p. 152).

In line with Freudian thinking what we have here is a cumulative stage
model, not a discrete stage, one in which later stages completely super-
sede earlier ones. Regression is an essential defence mechanism. On the
other hand this is an *epigenetic* theory in Erikson's terms. Jones explains
with emphases that

> all the psychological and social developments which are specific to each
> phase of the life cycle are, to a degree, predetermined by certain precursors
> in and certain derivatives from preceding phases of development, *and are*
> *also, to a degree, educable by virtue of the new possibilities for reorganisation offered*
> *by each succeeding phase of development* . . . In other words, to chart how a per-
> son's past has determined his present: it *may also be used predictively to chart*
> *how a person's present may both determine his future and redetermine his past*
> (Jones, 1968, p. 143–4).

Such are the nuclear growth crises. They are inevitable. There are also
accidental crises — Hamlet's whips and scorns of time — which are not
inevitable, but which occur in some measure to each one — anything from
absence to bereavement, insult to persecution, temporary indisposition to
crippling illness, loss of purse to loss of livelihood.

The individual must deal with each sort of crisis, the nuclear and the
accidental. This is done in Bruner's terms, by 'coping' or by 'defending'
though 'given the human condition neither coping nor defending is found
often in pure form' (Bruner, 1966, p. 129).

> Coping respects the requirements of problems we encounter while still
> respecting our integrity. Defending is a strategy whose objective is avoiding
> or escaping from problems for which we believe there is no solution that
> does not violate our integrity of functioning. Integrity of functioning is
> some level of self-consisting or style, the need to solve problems in a man-
> ner consistent with our most valued life enterprises.

Some of the most common defence mechanisms are: repression — a flat
refusal to face objective fact, though not as conscious behaviour; projection — where the blame for one's own faults is ascribed to someone else;
introjection — where we assume others' virtues and values; displacement
— where for example anger with one person may be redirected towards
another; rationisation — where an apparently rational explanation for
emotional behaviour is given; reaction formation — where the whole
behaviour is a defence against something unacceptable, a compensation;
sublimation — much less defensive than reaction formation, celibacy for
religious ends, for example; fantasy where reality is transformed by day-
dreaming; finally there is regression — where a person under stress
reverts to a less complex form of behaviour. All these mechanisms are
devices whereby we make life more tolerable for ourselves.

Regression is particularly important for our argument. Used in one sense the term refers to a clinical state; but in another it is common in everyday living. As Lowe (1972, p. xxiii) says:

> Psychoanalysts usually assume that no basic psychological crisis is ever fully resolved, and that traces of early partly resolved conflicts and partly satisfied needs will always persist into later life. If the frustration of early needs is a necessary part of living, then our tendency to regress to early developmental levels must be regarded as normal to precisely the same extent as the original frustration was inevitable. Such regressions cannot indicate abnormality. At most they represent a certain psychological vulnerability common to us all.

So much for defending. Effectively these devices are avoidance techniques. Coping on the other hand involves an acceptance that a problem exists and that one is responsible in relation to it. To accept that a problem exists is not the same as to accept the problem as such: people often cope by revaluing or redefining the elements of a situation. A basic mechanism in coping is the attempt to understand; but success is also related to the comparative success with which the earlier nuclear life crises have been solved.

The importance of the crisis model is that it focuses our attention on the validity of attitude and action at any point in life. Mature (crisis-coping) behaviour is not the same in the young as the old, nor are the nuclear crises, though the accidental ones may be. Maturity in this sense is being wise in your condition.

Organic sensibility

The education of the emotions, then, consists largely (to requote Peters) in the 'development of appraisals of the sort which are appropriate in terms of moral and aesthetic criteria and which are founded in realistic beliefs about how we are placed'. It was Wordsworth who said that poetry is the spontaneous overflow of powerful feelings: but not just that, for it requires long and deep thought along with more 'organic sensibility' than usual. He expresses the interrelationship as follows (Wordsworth, 1800, p. 223).

> For our continuing influxes of feelings are modified and directed by our thoughts, which are indeed the representation of all our past feelings; and as by contemplating the relation of these general representatives to each other, we discover what is really important to men, so by the repetition and continuance of this act feelings connected with important subjects will be nourished, till at length, if we be originally possessed by much organic sensibility, such habits of mind will be produced that by obeying blindly and mechanically the impulse of these habits we shall describe objects and other sentiments of such a nature and in such connection with each other, that the understanding of the being to whom we address ourselves, be in some degree enlightened, his taste exalted, his affections ameliorated.

The term 'organic sensibility' we could translate as the quality of feeling. Wordsworth is writing in 1800 at the end of a half century obsessed by the term 'sensibility', meaning a sensitivity to the delicate nuances of experience — one's own feelings and the feelings of others, including non-human creatures, and to the natural world. But Wordsworth means more than this. He is explicitly speaking about a response which is also informed by reason.

Let us try to define this organic sensibility further. First, it consists of 'right impulses', established by primary socialisation, and for that matter poetry: Wordsworth speaks of 'habits of mind' which become stabilised. The most fundamental of these is that all human beings are individuals and have rights by virtue of being human beings. Thus murder, rape, cannibalism, tyranny and slavery deny these rights; so do making use of people, emotional blackmail, humiliation. Second, there is the ability not merely to express one's feelings but to have awareness of their nature. Third, there is the ability to empathise with, to understand, other human beings. Fourth, there is the ability to relate to the environment: the natural world and the constructed world. Fifth, there is the ability to deal with nuclear life crises, and with the various accidental crises in the coping/defending modality. To a greater or lesser degree this involves cognition — to perceive, relate, distance, the complex factors involved.

'Organic sensibility', or any other model for the affect, will have a basis in a moral universe, assuming a general value system against which specific judgements are made. Because it makes judgements it will inhere in a cognitive world. It will be able to comment on the display of self, others, the natural and constructed environment, and on stances towards the human condition. The judgements will, on the one hand, rely on prior knowledge as a frame of reference, on the other on the quality of apprehension of the issues involved — degree of complexity, hierarchy of factors. For convenience we may set out the model in the form of a table (Table 2).

Application to writing

This approach leads us to read the compositions of younger writers with questions like the following in mind.

What general values are implied? In a multi-cultural society we can by no means assume uniformity. What specific moral judgements are made?
How far is the writer self-aware, and aware of the motivations of those written about as real individuals or story characters?
How far is the writer aware of, reacting to, making use of, the meaning of the environment?

Table 2: Organic sensibility, the affective model

Experience	Process	
Nuclear growth crises e.g. identity/diffusion: intimacy/isolation: generativity/stagnation.	*Values*	i. the moral structure of the universe. ii. specific value judgements
Incidental crises and departures from the ordinary.	*People*	i. self-becoming aware (motives, context, image) of self ii. self — becoming aware of neighbour as self — of others
	Environment:	self — becoming aware of, interacting with
	Reality	i. personal stance — the established 'impulse of habits' ii. cognitive stance — the use of defending and coping strategies

How far are the writer's appraisals positive and 'acceptable'?
How 'mature' are the writer's responses to problem and crisis?

The questions will be further defined, and answers to them explored, in subsequent chapters.

Comment

In this chapter the education of the affect has been considered as being a matter of cognition and morals as well as feeling. A concept, 'organic sensibility' in Wordsworth's terms, seems to describe the 'quality of feeling'. This is related to a psychoanalytical theory of human development as a preliminary to specifying the sort of questions we should ask about writing.

6 The human condition

Coping and defending

Ostriches do not bury their heads in the sand, contrary to popular belief. If they did they would suffocate, as a moment's reflection will enable us to see. Nevertheless the expression is a useful one to describe us when we will not face facts, and 'defend' ourselves against the more demanding aspects of living. This is often necessary in the short term for all of us since the stress of confronting problems is painful, but if it becomes a way of life it puts us out of touch with reality. The opposite term, in common use, is 'coping' or 'managing', which means facing problems rather than avoiding them. The two terms 'coping' and 'defending' are used by psychologists to describe two approaches to life as we find it (Bruner, 1966, pp. 129–30).

The belief about ostriches arises from medieval traveller' tales and fables. Fables are monumental lies containing spiritual truths. The animal fables from the sixth century BC, associated with the name of Aesop, are almost a psychologist's manual on 'coping and defending', many expressions from which have come down to us. Aesop's particular brand of 'coping' is that of a cautious realist — pride goes before a fall, make haste slowly, God helps those who help themselves, be careful whom you trust, and above all see where power lies and make your pact with it before it destroys you.

The fables on 'defending' are also highly perceptive. In fact one of them, about the fox who, unable to reach the grapes, then calls them 'sour', provides us with the classic example of *rationalisation*. *Regression*, a reversion to more primitive behaviour under emotion, is seen in another famous story of the man who kills the goose that lays the golden eggs believing there is a store of gold inside her. Here his thinking has regressed. An example of *introjection* — claiming merit due to others — is seen in the fly sitting on the coach wheel who says 'What a dust I am raising'. In contrast, *projection* is assigning one's own faults to others, as in Aesop's doctor who blames his patient for dying instead of blaming himself for the

67

advice he failed to give. *Displacement* is seen in the fable of the serving maids whose mistress gets them up early and who take their frustration out on the cock and kill it. (This fails in that the mistress, not now knowing when dawn is, gets the maids up in the middle of the night.)

One of the most common defence mechanisms is *fantasy*. The frog imagines she is as large as the ox, and when they tell her she is not she puffs herself out till she explodes. The tortoise believes she could fly as well as the eagle, if only she had a chance. The eagle tries to convince her otherwise, but when she insists he takes her to a dizzy height; she falls to the rocks and is smashed to pieces. A frog announces that he is a great doctor, but the fox says he can't even cure his own lameness. A cat takes on the part of a princess so beautifully that she deceives people and marries a prince. Unfortunately a mouse runs across the floor at their wedding feast, and her true nature is revealed. All these fantasy ways of living eventually prove useless or even disasterous.

A revised model

With this background we can turn to 'coping' and 'defending' as expressed in more up-to-date terms, for convenience tabulated below. In the previous chapter we argued that the quality of feeling in writing needed to be looked at, not in the abstract but in a variety of situations, involving the self, one of which was in relation to the 'human condition'. Suggestions were made in the original Crediton project how this might be done, but they were tentative, and subsequent work (Curtis, 1982; Worsley, 1983) has developed a more soundly-based scheme. The figure code (A4, etc.) refers to the section in the original Crediton model which this now replaces.

A4   The human condition
       The writer shows awareness of the reality of the human condition. He uses a variety of devices to defend his position in relation to the world of people and events, or he shows his ability to cope with reality in positive ways.

A4.1   Gives a literal account without evaluation.

A4.2   *Defending*
       (i)   *Repression.* A flat refusal to accept a demonstrable fact.
       (ii)   *Regression.* Reversion to earlier form of behaviour (e.g., tantrums).
       (iii)   *Displacement.* An emotion redirected (e.g., frustration at work taken out on family).
       (iv)   *Rationalisation.* Apparently reasonable and acceptable explanation for an attitude (e.g., sour grapes).
       (v)   *Introjection.* Assuming other's qualities (e.g., claiming credit/responsibility due to others).

(vi) *Fantasy*. Creation of unreal solutions as in daydreams, ideal outcomes.

(vii) *Projection*. Assigning own faults to others.

A4.3   Coping

(i) *Recognition* A recognition that the problem exists with no attempt at 'defence' against it: a statement with no or little understanding.

(ii) *Problem solved*

   (a) in terms of conventional wisdom ('love will find a way', 'forgive and forget'). A simple, completed solution.

   (b) in terms of specific action or event, e.g., change of environment produces new situation.

(iii) *Partial solution*. A modification or amelioration of the situation.

(iv) *In perplexity*. An appreciation of the complexities of a problem, demonstrating insight into it, but recognising there can be no (immediate) or simple solution. Coming to terms.

Realistic situations

It has been found in various 'Crediton studies' that the topic of an 'adolescent problem' is helpful in eliciting self-defining meaningful compositions from young writers in that age group (Curtis, 1982; Worsley, 1983; Bidwell, 1985). The formulation used by Worsley (1983, p. 85) was 'Write a story, real or imaginary, which concerns a teenage problem and involves a realistic solution'. The writings analysed below were elicited by Kulsdom (1985).

The sample used was the 104 scripts from five fifth-year English classes in a mixed comprehensive school drawing on a multi-racial community. Certain themes dominated irrespective of the culture of the writers. Almost half were concerned with relationships with and between parents; a quarter with drugs and glue sniffing; a small number with the problems of parties, pregnancy, abortion; a few with mixed relationships. It was expected that there would be scripts on two apparent preoccupations of these students — examinations and unemployment — but it seems that the word 'problem' did not convey these topics, or alternatively that they were anxious about certain topics. As one girl said on tape later, 'I think a lot of people are worrying about their exams; it may be they don't want to express their feelings'. Of unemployment a boy said: 'Just scares you, don't it?' The task was administered by the teachers of the classes and not by the experimenter, and it is likely that their suggestion of 'teenage problems' influenced the choices. A persistent question was 'What do you mean by a problem?' Some of the problems are clearly outside the experience of the writers, for which we may be thankful: one girl who wrote about VD had got her information from social education lessons. Clearly much of the drugs, sex and crime came from TV. The question reminded one girl of the 'problem page'. The conclusion to be drawn is not that teenagers do not have problems, particularly the problems adults feel it obligatory for them to have, but that the word 'problem' so popular in educational circles did not indicate to these adolescents their own perplexities.

The predominant problem written about was relationships with parents. Rebecca depicts a situation of no understanding in which rage replaces communication (A4.2(ii)). 'Sallie' is accused of coming in late:

> 'For gods sake Sallie, you are only fifteen, how old do you think you are bloody twenty one?'
> Fifteen! yes that is my age I realise that so why can't you? she screamed ... 'Dad, I am not a baby no more I am growing up can't you see that? I want to go out and enjoy myself. You are only young once you know'

The writer comments that the father 'can not cope' with the growing independence of his daughter; there is no evidence that she is distanced from this situation. 'Kevin' is in the same situation. He comes in late and finds unexpectedly his father waiting up for him:

> 'I didn't realise the time!'
> 'Don't give me that, don't you think I worry?'
> 'I can look after myself'
> 'I'm only trying to help you!'
> 'Yes', Kevin replied while pushing past his father 'You could have fooled me'.

However there are indications that the writer is not to be equated completely with Kevin. The title is 'Friend or Foe?'. The father states his point of view, and Kevin's behaviour 'pushing past his father' is not presented uncritically; there are the beginnings of 'coping' here, whereby the writer defines the problem realistically (A4.3(i)) though he is far away from any resolution of it.

However there were also writers able to be more objective about the problems and see them as associated with a particular stage. Linda calls her piece 'Careing Parents', and describes a girl who 'finely got chucked out of school her mum and dad could not controll her so she was put into a home'. The conclusion is in the form of a comment on the incident.

> Karen could not see that her mum and dad were just trying to help her in the first place being hard on her so that she would not get hert or fall into the bad company that some kids do. When Karen gets older she will have kids and worrey about them the way her parents have for her.

Conventional solutions can imply a certain passivity. Other writers described solutions brought about by rational action rather than by waiting on events. Commonly the parents who object to an unknown boyfriend are won round after meeting him. 'Irene' describes a girl who talks over the matter of her freedom with her parents and was given more, and 'never took advantage of it, never' (A4.3(ii)(b)). In Anne's piece, 'Karen's parents say to her (A4.3(ii)(b)):

> Karen we have seen how happy you are being fancy free so your mother and I have decided to let you out with this boy on a regular basis as long as he brings you home at a reasonable time.
> 'Oh mum, dad, thank you' Karen kissed them and went to bed. Karen's problems with her parents were solved'.

In two other compositions the boyfriend charms the mother into submission.

If such outcomes seem perhaps slightly oversimplified the same cannot be said of those in a few of the scripts like Isabel's. 'Tracy' and her father abuse one another when she comes home late in a tension aggravated by the fact that her mother has left home. Tracy sympathises with her mother, but a dream indicated she also has feelings for her father's plight. She dreams of her childhood in which they were all three playing together.

> Suddenly her mother was gone from the picture and it was just her father as he was now. She wasn't in the part any more but in a strange home with her father siting in his chair, his face in his hands. Slowly she went up to him touched his shoulder.
> 'What's wrong' she asked slowly.
> 'Vera's dead —'

It is as though the dream had been shared for in the morning he seems brighter, and she is surprised he speaks to her nicely. He asks her to open a letter from her mother:

> Tracy opened the letter and began to read to herself first
>   What does it say? her father asked.
> 'O not much, just that she's sorry and how we're doing'
>   She folded the letter up. Her father was standing over a frying pan and didn't say anything. Tracy felt angry, but also sorry for her Dad
> 'Dad?'
> 'Eggs. Tracy?' he asked.

Tracy's complex and ambiguous feelings, the *possible* hint of a reconciliation 'she's sorry', her father's gesture of love symbolised by 'Eggs. Tracy?' indicate no glib or speedy solution but the need to make small gains, to wait, to tolerate uncertainties (A4.3(iv)).

Another piece with similar complexity is concerned, apparently trivially, with a girl whose isolation is made worse by her acne and is persecuted by her classmates as 'acne face'. She is defended by the writer who stands up to the bullies and succeeds in obtaining some peace for her. There is no pretence that everything is magically transformed, but some things have improved (A4.3(iii):

> She is certainly the same boring girl with acne but at best Janet doesnt bother her any more, and I think Sally's happy that way.

In the piece about Tracy the outcome is the result in effect of the assessment of the situation so as to be aware of its dimensions. Ranjit, from India, does the same in a piece called 'Living with Guardians' which gives a brief history and background, describes the circumstances, and refers to the constraints. Nevertheless there are advantages:

> People living with various guardians gain more experience of life than the others and this experience can lead them through all the hardships of life which lies in future. I hope that someday I will find all this hardship useful to face the problems of life.

The culture of the writer is doubtless a factor in a situation where one might have expected protest and rejection A4.3(ii)(a)).

Naturally many of the writers feel the need for a complete solution to the problem they discuss, and they resort to conventional wisdom to conclude their stories: experience teaches; forgive and forget; virtue is rewarded; vice is punished; there are more fish in the sea; love will find a way; time heals; deus ex machina. Some examples follow.

Vicky describes 'Gemma', 14, 'quiet and never really got into serious trouble' who moved schools and 'got in with the wrong crowd' and began to smoke, drink and take drugs. She went to a party against her parent's wishes, took drugs, and was taken to hospital 'near to dying', having been rescued by her father. She has learned her lesson (A4.3(ii)(a)).

> She told her parents she wouldn't be taking any more drugs and that she wouldn't be seeing her so-called friend again. She thought of herself just laying in that comer, nearly dead, and none of the friend had card about her.
>   Now she is going to another school. She has dyed her hair her own colour and doesn't wear as much make up and jewellery. Her attitude has also changed. She is back to her old self and thats the way her parents like it.

Les depicts 'David' and his friend seeing a skinhead collapse from drugs: 'It taught me and Dave a lesson'. In Robert's story a belief in restitution and forgiveness is displayed. A boy working in a sweet shop finds the money 'sitting in the till, staring at me full in the face begging me to take it'. He succumbs to temptation: the owner finds out and tells his parents. He is forgiven as long as he repays the money and promises no recurrence:

It was very lucky for me that I had a good boss as I would have been walking the street now looking for a job.

In contrast Ross tells us of 'Jack' 'stuck on cocane' who robs family, friends and eventually a bank, to sustain the habit. He is caught on film record and receives '14 month jail'.

Other conventional solutions are represented, for instance, by authority. 'Joseph' and 'Frank' are bullied by having their heads flushed in school toilets. They complain to the head who expells the bullies. The girl in Gail's story, whose boyfriend comes back five years after their baby was born, seems set for a happy ending — 'and lived happy ever after' — but then comments:

> but Remember learn by my mistake never go to bed with a boy even if you use the equipment cause it is an unpleasant experience.

Experience teaches (A4.3(ii)) as it does Gemma, a potential drug addict, and Claire, rejected by her boyfriend when it seemed as if the whole world was ending, but 'as my friend said there's plenty more fish in the sea'. Laurie, facing an immense onslaught from his fuming mother having been out late with a girl, asked himself 'all this for a girl was it worth it'.

These conventional solutions are 'coping' solutions in that they are at least possible. When solutions become improbable, almost magical, we have to regard them as 'defending'. In 'The boys in blue' David describes how a policeman wrongly arrests young sales manager for stabbing a tramp. Just as things look very black it appears the policeman has been arrested for harrassment and all charges are dropped. In 'The Disco' Celestine depicts 'Denise' bringing her boyfriend home: her parents are shocked that he is black. He tells them: 'I love your daughter very much, as she loves me and feel that with love as strong as ours we will make it work'. The final comment is:

> They stayed very happily married until they both died after 60 years of happiness. It goes to show that if youve got the strength to make it it can work.

Mario tells the story of 'Andrew' who has a speech blockage, but he stayed at home and developed an ability to write poetry and made a good living, so that, although he couldn't speak, 'he made communication with about 40% of every living person in the world'. Amul depicts a boy beaten by bullies. A man advises him not to fear their size — 'the bigger they are the heavier they fall' — and gives him a 'poction' saying it was 'goast milk and sugar and faith'. The writer gives us no indication of the outcome or whether he views the advice as metaphorical (A4.2(vi)).

Some problems, such as those of sexual relations, produce as one would expect, a wide range of treatment. 'Barry' and his girlfriend are pleasantly surprised to find her parents think her unintended pregnancy is 'great' and they were soon able to save up and buy a house (Karen). In

a similar situation 'Julie' and 'Alan' are bought a house as a wedding present, and the mothers serve as babysitters so that the couple are not incon-
venienced. Christopher depicts a 15-year-old girl becoming pregnant at
a drugs party. Her boyfriend accepts her baby by someone else

> I am precancy o who done it to you that boy in that club we went to we got
> to have the baby now.

Other stories include abortion but it is not represented as very satisfactory. Under pressure from the boyfriend, John, and her parents, 'Lisa'
'has an abortion, but even so splits with John, after a hard time having killed their own child and having done a wrong thing'. The writer condemns
girls who 'don't even know they are going to get pregnant and don't take
precautions, and thus throw away their chance of education and a degree'.

The most aware account is that of Jayne: 'Clair' is forced to have sex
and becomes pregnant. She analyses her feelings towards the boy and
herself; and considers her plans — to have the baby adopted, to return to
her parents — but they might not want her. She wishes to start again —
but asks whether that is possible:

> She would get it adopted and after would go home and explain all to her
> parents and if they would allow her to she would slowly, but carefully try
> and pick her life together, it would be hard but somehow she knew in the
> end she would succeed. But that experience would be in her for the rest of
> her born days, but somehow she didn't hate Delray or his colour, it was her-
> self that she hated, she knew she had been unlucky to meet him and have
> such a dismile experience she would just try and forget him and she would
> have to start life all over again, the question was 'could she?'

We have here a 'coping' with the problem which does not attempt to
diminish its doubtful features and complexities (A4.3(iv)).

In a few pieces, Leroy's in particular, there is no defending, no solution,
only a bleak contemplation which is producing confusion and despair.

> I went home at 8.25. 'Where have you been?' said my dad
>   'Out with Gary'.
>   'Look I don't whant you going out when it's dark'.
>   'It's not dark'. I sat down and watched TV, my dad followed.
>   Look 'I'm not letting you stay out al night' said dad
>   'It's only half eight'.
>   'It's dark'
>   'It's not dark' I said
>   'Play, play, play, thats all you do'.
>   'I do my work'
>   'Where?'
>   'At school'.
>   'At school' Then dad turned away to watch TV shaking his head from
> side to side. I hate when he does that. It like that with my dad. 'When I get
> home work I do it' I said.

'But I never see you'

'Your at work when I do it'.

It like that with everything. I go out with a girl called Angela she's 16 and I go swimming with her. I go about 9.00 am to about 5.30 pm and my dad still mones. I'll tell you something I got so confeused once I tried to commit sewiside. I've got a few friends but not a real friend. I DON'T KNOW WHAT TO DO.

The story is marked 'Fact', and indeed this is strongly suggested anyway by the accuracy of the dialogue and the realism of the details — the habitual headshaking of his father which the boy finds particularly irritating. This is not defending — in no sense does he the writer try to avoid the problem. In fact he faces it, but no solution is in sight. In effect he cries out for help (A4.3(i)). (Fortunately other information enabled the school to begin to help this boy.)

Several of the writers show awareness of defending strategies in the behaviour of characters in their stories. Becky depicts 'Julie's' mother as resisting her bringing her boyfriend home, but then realising later that her hostility to him has been partly jealousy of youth:

I just didn't want you to go on enjoying yourself because I was jealous of you being young.

(Rationalisation, A4 2(iv)). Joanna attributes 'Tony's' delinquent behaviour to neglect at home and thus in effect a revenge on his parents, and at the same time a demand for their notice (A4 2(iii)). This leads in effect to his death by drugs:

Tony fell to the ground. He was no more. Now he would be noticed.

The mother of 'Diane', in Jenny's story 'Mothers', is interpreted as dominating her family because of her own neglect in a large family as a child.

Diane's mother was considered as an easy woman to get on with, socially, but where her sons, daughters and even her husband was concerned, she would be the judge or magistrate and have the last word. She was only 39 but she weighed 17 stone and looked like Nelly the elephant. Diane's mother was brought up with 8 brothers and 4 sisters which made her feel that she would give her children as much love and care as they need.

The aspect of coping whereby the writer seeks metaphors as an 'objective correlative' is well demonstrated here. The mother is a 'judge' or 'magistrate' and, despite her comparative youth, her dominance is represented in the simile of an elephant.

Fictional situations

A study by Worsley (1983) examined the compositions of further education students in response to an 'adolescent problem', and to two fictional dilemmas. One is concerned with the child of Jehovah's Witnesses who, in the doctor's opinion, needed a blood transfusion to save her life. The other, concerning a heart transplant, is discussed here.

The participants, students between 16 and 19 years of age, taking a variety of academic and occupational courses, were given the following written formulation of the assignment:

Information
A team of doctors has been given the difficult task of deciding which of two patients will receive the next heart transplant, when a heart is available. Neither patient will survive long without treatment. The patients are:
Anne, 12 years old, the only child of an electrician and his wife; Mark, aged 48, an executive and the father of four children.

Task
Write a story based on this information for a magazine; use your imagination to create characters, setting a story for the situation.

This is not an English test; just do you best with spelling, punctuation etc.
Try and give your story a title.
Length does not matter but try to write a *complete* story.

The writers were given a choice and 13 undertook this assignment.

The dilemma presented here is a very cruel one, and not one that mercifully the vast majority of people are called upon to face, though in the medical profession decisions of this order, if not in these terms, are by no means uncommon. Not surprisingly, therefore, despite the apparent necessity to make a decision, ten out of the 13 writers used some form of escape from doing so. In three no decision was attempted, in five one of the patients died before tramsplant was possible. In another Mark made his own decision — that he has been fortunate and had a good life and should now sacrifice his own life to save that of the child. In yet another two hearts became unexpectedly available. A typical comment when one of the patients died was:

It is a relief in some ways to realise that the heart would never have reached the 48 year old patient in time to save his life.

When a decision was made justification was felt to be needed, and other factors were built in, making it more desirable to save one life than another, because of family circumstances or other medical problems. In one piece Mark was verging on alcoholism. Feelings of guilt were evident in these pieces, for instance on the part of Anne when she discovered her life had been saved at the expense of Mark's, and on the part of a doctor who dramatises the issue:

he would be a murderer, even if they did not consider him a murderer it would be on his conscience for ever.

In fact the attempt to empathise with the characters in the story was notable. What obviously could not be appreciated by these writers was the essentially professional attitude of surgeons in dilemmas of this nature. Taken in personal terms the choice would be overwhelming, and thus it is not surprising that aspects of defending, particularly rationalisation and fantasy, dominated the responses.

Yet we may justly ask what is the source of these convenient solutions and the answers may lie in one model provided by romantic fiction. It will be recalled that the students were asked to write a story 'for a magazine' and the provenance of Marie's story (style, characterisation and sentiments) will be clear from the following extract. The surgeon is narrator:

> Mark, was rather like me, or should I say, what I thought was me. He was steady as a rock, a ruthless executive who had made it to the top by sheer guts! But he smoked twenty a day, drank an awful lot of scotch and ate all the wrong things. He got his first heart attack at forty-two and, despite vigorous dieting, cutting down on the smoking and drinking, he was deteriorating fast. I admired the man greatly, he knew what was happening to himself and yet, he had four children and a devoted wife. He was the perfect father, always there when the boys needed advice, and for his girls there was a sholder to cry upon if they needed it.
>
> Why me? Why did I have to make that decision? There was a knock on the door and Mark walked in. He nodded curtly as he sat down.
>
> "Can I help you Mark?" I enquired. He then informed me of a decision that he had made, a decision that had been made by one of the most unselfish, bravest men I had ever met. He told me that he had decided not to have the operation even if the heart was available as he felt sure that there was somebody who needed it more than he did. He was fourty-eight, he's reached the top, he'd got a beautiful family.
>
> "But why guarantee your death, you've got everything to live for!" I felt my voice drifting off.
>
> "I've made my decision, my family are well provided for, they know as well as I do what will happen to me with this decision, All I propose to do is to enjoy the rest of my life – I'm taking my family away for a short period. I would like to thank you for all you've done Doctor."

However, some of the other writings of this group of students, in response to the 'teenage problem', show them very critical of romance solutions. Robert's story of a marriage enforced by pregnancy has the girl commenting:

> Yeh, how bloody romantic — I didn't read about this in Mills and Boon.

Curtis (1982) asked a group of late- teenaged boys and girls to give a narrative response to a Canadian anti-drink poster, depicting an adolescent girl alone, slumped in a chair. Her schoolbooks are on the floor and she contemplates what seems to be whisky in a glass she is holding. One writer's response is in the form of a monologue:

What did John say to me? I put too much into myself and not enough towards others — or something like that. Well, anyway, I was just about to break off with him . . . I think. Who am I trying to fool? I really liked him. But he doesn't like me. I guess nobody does. May as well chalk up another victory to my smashing ability to alienate others while disturbing my own peace of mind. As far as I can see, I have two choices. I could do as "dear" old dad said and act like a lady instead of some classy snob. Mommy dearest added to dad's idea by saying "I never acted like that when *I* was your age". If they care for me so much where are they now? Away on another of dad's business trips. Well, I don't mind, it gives me a chance to just sit here with my drinks and think about my other option. Mom can't scream at me now about "teenage alcoholics" and "what happens to girls like you", In fact, maybe she never will again. What's the name of that Quinlan one? Kathleen? No, that's the name of the actress. Karen Ann, I believe. I think she mixed some type of drug or something with her booze. A bottle of aspirin should do it, if I'm not too drunk to go to the medicine cabinet and get it. I'll get it after this drink . . . along with a pen and paper. Bye mom, bye dad, what else . . . Oh Yeah, dear John, I'm gone Ha-ha. Minglewood couldn't have said it better. Heres looking at you kid, down the hatch.

Here of course is the adolescent nuclear identity crisis. Her assessment of the view of others towards her ('nobody likes me') is presumably the expected exaggeration, and there is projection of blame onto parents ('It's other people to blame'. 'I am being victimised'). Her assessment that there are only two choices open to her is an avoidance mechanism (A4.2(iv) & (v)).

This piece raises in very interesting form that role of the narrator. Sometimes the writer portrays the narrator as a character in the writing. And this is what happens here. The girl expresses regressive punitive and self-pitying attitudes. But the writer is in fact a boy, Micky, who is, in that way at least, distanced from her. There are, however, other signs of distancing, not least his ability to portray a girl in the register — 'dear', 'old dad', 'classy snob', 'mommy dearest'. In an ability to portray immaturity we have an indicator of maturity.

Comment

The insights of these writers are by no means necessarily related to their literary ability, but arise as they seek their own particular wisdoms. Many of them are aware of the various mechanisms of defending, particularly in others. Parents are shown as refusing to face the growing independence of their children, (A4.2(i)), both sides resorting to tantrums and abuse (A4.2(ii)), taking out frustrations on others (A4.2(iii)), displaying self-deceit (A4.2(iv)). Fantasy is sometimes a solution (A4.2(vi)) particularly in romantic situations but it is rather the realism than the fantasy that prevails. The writers do not avoid so much as try to cope.

Coping is shown at first level in *acceptance*, a facing of the apparent facts of the situation, however unpleasant. Leroy finds this contemplation produces despair. There is no attempt to avoid the problem but no insight into it.

Next there is a group of solutions in which *popular wisdom* is found to provide a satisfactory interpretation. These tend to be passive rather than active — experience teaches (sometimes bitterly), restitution and forgiveness, virtue rewarded, vice punished, love triumphs, authority intervenes, there are more fish in the sea. Those are 'morals' to be drawn. Sometimes, however, there are no such obvious outcomes — perhaps *small gains* which modify aspects of a situation: the isolated girl with acne is helped but her problems do not go away because they are in her personality. Finally there are those copings which recognise the complex nature of experience, and its continuous nature, and realise that for some problems there are no simple or immediate solutions. A good example of this is Isabel's story about father and daughter left alone when the mother deserts. Usually such stories have in them a sensitive analysis of the characters and situation which is how a diagnosis comes to be made. The maturity of a response does not rely on an ability to come up with a solution, but rather on such factors as its insights, in its sense of complexity, of its imaginative grasp of the problem, as in Micky's piece about the despairing girl.

The role of fiction as an educational tool is an interesting one. We have seen that certain fictionalised problems tended to prompt defending solutions, and of course that one of the functions of fiction is to develop fantasy, ideal worlds which benefit us not by solving our problems, but by removing us from them. *Wuthering Heights* is about the disaster which arises from a man's passion for a married woman; nobody claims it solves our problems, and everybody, including bishops, enjoys it. What is much more significant is the fiction which is related to, or indeed which is part of, the everyday myths of society. Fiction as part of the reinforcement of such social myths is obviously not of continuous educational value, useful though it may be as escapism. Throughout human history the basic regression has always been to magical thinking, and this has been traditionally expressed in myths about miracles and divine interventions. Nothing has changed except the terms of the myths — not the pot of gold at the end of the rainbow but the pools bonanza at the beginning of the season.

7 Who are we?

Introduction

Writing helps us to understand ourselves and other people. We do not need to be writing about either in any obvious way. We could be reporting an incident in which we say how we felt at the time: or writing a story in which we discover understanding of the characters by having them behave in certain ways. In this chapter however we shall discuss compositions in which the writers quite specifically focus on themselves, and on others, asking in effect the questions: Who am I? and Who are you?

Who am I?

6–12–year-olds
In writing about 'Myself' young writers give three kinds of information. The first we might call *formal* — the sort that one might have to fill in on an official form — name, age, even weight, address, members of family, possessions. The second is information about *actions*; many of these actions are insignificant in describing us, such as going to school, or sleeping; others more significant — our achievements, crimes, oddities. A third class we may call *dispositional* items — describing our temperament, character, personality. Occurring so frequently as to be almost a sub-class with younger children are lists of likes and dislikes. Thus Charlie, aged six, develops this with riotous enthusiasm:

> I like banging my heDe a gast the wall and liyk Food I liyk School I liyk water I liyk news

An example containing all the times at a very simple level is by Scott:

> My name is Scott
> What I like best is doing sums
> I like playing football and I am six
> I am quite good and
> like this school

Unless they take Charlie's method of listing similar items the 4–6-year-olds have no organising principle and present information haphazardly as Scott does. This also applies to 7–8-year-olds. However the latter are on the whole much more fluent and feel the need to write more. This additional material takes the form of chronicle or narrative. A typical piece, by Tom (6.11),is given below:

> Halow my name is Tom and I have a brouther and a sistder my brouther is called Glen my sister is called Lynne. I have a mummy and a Daddy. and no I will well you a sorty adalt Saterday and Sunday. (There follows a chronicle of domestic happenings on both days.)

The narrative pull is so strong with some children that it obviates any attempt to write about 'myself'. Wendy (7) begins 'Once there was a nice teacher' and follows this by a long chronicle of insignificant items which includes the dentist, but ends by Wendy and her mum giving a birthday party to the teacher.

Young children's writing about themselves, then, consists overwhelmingly of formal items, actions including achievements, and dispositional items of the positive preference kind (I like). Dispositional items of general qualities (beyond 'nice') are rare. Where they are more extended the extensions will tend to be chronicles which do not, except accidentally, illustrate features of the self of the writer. Usually there will be no principle of organisation apparent, and this goes with a lack of unity in the persona presented. In one writer only in our sample was there an approach to coherence. Heidi (8.1) concentrates predominantly on the things which make her 'go mad' and even in places attempts to account for these:

> about me
>
> When I do something wrong it makes me go mad. In assembly we sing songs the best son I like is when I needed a neighbour. Some days I don't want to come to school because I an too tired. When my mum says "Shall we go to the shops to by something with your pocket money", I say "do we have to". "Because I don't want to walk". Then it makes me go really mad. Because it makes my legs ache. Sometimes my mum untiedes my desk at home and I like to keep my desk neat. If I have liver for tea it makes me go mad because I don't like liver. When I can play with Danielle I feel Happy because I have got someone to play with. When I go swimming I feel very Happy. 8 years old.

It is significant that Heidi uses the word 'because' five times. It distinguishes her from other writers in the sample who do not account for the feelings and preferences that they record.

With 10–11-year-olds in our sample a new element enters into the descriptions — some attempt at objectivity about the self, manifest in an awareness that others might have a viewpoint about the writer not corresponding to the writer's own. David (11.1) writes about himself in the third

person (though not consistently) including dispositional items like
'doesn't have a very god temper' and notes a deeper self than the surface
appearance indicates: 'He works quite average, but he can work quite
heard when he want to'. The objectifying device used by several children
is a letter from one teacher to another about the writer. Alan (11), on the
other hand, uses the expectations of others for this purpose:

> I am Alan Bader and aged 11. A bad point about me is I don't fit into the
> person my family would like me to be, my parents would like me to be a
> president or prime-minister but I would like to make living as something
> dangerous or adventeres like a stuntman or actor. Another bad point is I
> like to get out of situations I don't like. A good point about me is I am very
> careful about what I say & what I do and I always chose my own disitions.

The type of classificatory system and the strongly self-critical stance is
one we have not encountered so far.

More writers at this age try to present a unified persona. Ian speaks of
a tendency towards depression and attempts to arrange information
around this theme; he is aware of the difference between private self and
public presentation:

> I haven't been very well lately and was very depressed but I tried to be happy
> to everyone else wouldn't be depressed.

Justin does not equate the self with the action like the younger children
did. There is a self, and the self can act in a variety of ways:

> I try to think before I act and the reason when I do something rong nobody
> else gets the blame.
> I do what I believe its no use doing something that is against your belief.
> I never go into things I don't understand I would get in more mess that
> I started.

Justin tried to express his sense of reflexion as 'two minds'.

> I try to think from to minds as if I was two people.

For Danny self-knowledge is difficult:

> As I write about myself or someone I think it is impossible to be one
> hundred persent honest

He has a sense of the self that has been conferred on him by others:

> I do have a good name from family and people at my school but it takes a
> lot of time and pationts to build that type of likeness up.

and a sense of the gap between potential and performance:

> I could do better is a hard working way.

13–18-year-olds
With 13-year-olds the impression one receives of most immediate difference from the writings of the younger children is the increased use of

dispositional items — words like 'understanding', 'embarrassment', 'anxiety', 'trust', 'relaxed', 'sympathetic', 'arrogant', 'loyal', 'friendly', are noted commonly. The task given by Bidwell (1985) to adolescents (aged 13–18) was 'Write a description of yourself as seen by a friend and also by a person who does not like you'. The appearance of a vocabulary for the emotions confirms the original Crediton assessment that the affective development of the individual moves from an expression of feeling to an awareness of feeling and to an understanding of feeling. The less-developed writing tends to describe individuals in terms of externals. Joanne's friend thinks that she has big feet (size 4) and blond hair which 'looks pretty in a side parting' while her 'enemy' thinks her hair is 'as straight as a beanpole' and she should 'get a brace for her teeth as soon as possible'.

The distancing and objectivity required by the question was beyond many writers. With them things were very much black and white; Frank assumes one person will praise him, and the other will abuse him:

> (my friend) thinks that I am a really great goal keeper
> (my enemy) would think I am a big monkey and a tory idiot.

Self-analysis was also avoided by a considerable defensiveness which came out in a comic self-mockery. Dick writes:

> My enemies say I look like a spudgy toad. Some say I am a flat frog . . . Some say I am a lanky legged curly locked bigfoot.

On the whole, however, both at 13 and 17 the scripts reveal serious, sometimes painful, self-examination: the 'friend' is represented usually as being by no means uncritical. On the other hand, the person who does not like the writer often takes up the same point as the friend but gives it a different slant: Jane, according to friends, is sociable:

> and if I was asked to go to a party . . . I would jump at the chance.

To the observer this makes Jane a 'tart', to which she cannot resist replying 'compared with her I'm a 'snob''. Her friends know Jane to be anxious about examinations and certain meetings: her enemies say 'she'd worry about having nothing to worry about'. To her friends Maria works particularly hard in every subject except maths and geography, and especially hard in French and German. But a different view of this is

> She's rubbish at Geography but a creep in French and German.

There is no absolute relationship between age and apparent maturity in the writing, but one of the most developed pieces is in fact by a 17-year-old, Adam. He recognises the validity of different views of himself — his own, his girlfriend's and that of someone who does not care for him. But he also knows that the perceptions of observers may be conditioned by views they think the observed have of them:

He thinks I hate him and that is probably one of the reasons why he hates me. He seems to be jealus of me and my luck in many ways but would die before admitting it.

He can examine the images he presents to the world — 'collected and thoughtful maturity' to his friends, 'arrogant and conceited' to his enemies. His girlfriend he sees as not accepting his weaknesses but tolerating them:

Despite the superficial image of 'hardness' and insensitive behaviour she knows there is a thoughtful and spriritual person in me.

And he does not attempt to discount the adverse views of the enemy merely because of their source, but recognises they may be correct. What makes the difference is the attitude accompanying the perception. If this is unfavourable, then it breeds further dislike which does not confine itself to its first object only:

Again he knows I'm impulsive and dislikes me for it. He thinks I talk too much and show off. In many ways he is right about my weaknesses but hates me not solely because of them. He doesn't dislike only me however, he dis-likes friends of mine as well.

To conclude this section we may quote from the work of another 17-year-old responding to the topic 'Myself'. Here we find John able to take an overview, seeing his problems at any one time as being in part a result of a combination of local factors. So he makes a statement of his correct belief:

At the age that I am at at the moment I believe there could be no harder time. I have to go out and find a job that will satisfy me for the rest of my life.

and then qualifies it, indicating an awareness of his place in time — he is conscious that the current situation is not necessarily the only situation:

At all the points and times in my life where I have had problems, I have always believed they would be the worst times I'll ever have.

He has a consciousness of the different forms of mental activity:

At the moment I believe that as soon as I get a job all my big problems will be gone. Maybe that's more hope than belief. . . .
    I sometimes wonder if I would and could be a good adult. My pride likes to think so, but my reason, weighing up my pros and cons tells me I am not. . . .

He is able to look at himself with fair objectivity, in contrast to the self-centred views of some of his contemporaries.

I believe I have my bad points like stubbornness and on some occasions a short temper. But I also have my good points. I have a sense of humour and an opinion on life which is fairly elastic, and I also believe in other people. Some people my age believe the world rotates round them.

Who are you?

6–9-year-olds

In describing other people known to them (the title 'My best friend' or a 'Friend of mine' was offered), young children not surprisingly use the same categories as when writing about themselves. Thus we have found details (name, age, and so on) physical description (colour of hair, eyes, and so on), actions and achievements, and preferences (or detestations). Caroline's biography of her friend written as a letter from her teacher displays all these characteristics:

> Her name is caroline and she is 9 years old. She got brown hair and brown eyes and dark skin. She takes size three in shoes. She has two brother and one dog.
> She is good at maths language and danceing. She has been at ballet for five years. She dose ballet moden and tap. She dose ballet on Saturdays. Moden on Wednesday and Tap on Fridays. She quiet good at Swiming. She is on her yellow.
> She does not like people kicking her in the leg and she dose-not like people poking her in the neck. She said she doeset like people tickling under her arms.

Formal items are common, even obsessively so: Clare amongst others gives the height, weight, address and postcode and phone number of her friend. So are preferences. Penny gives us Caron's favourite food — chips:

> Her worst food is Green.

Miscellaneous residential and dental information is also given by Caron.

> She lives in a bungalow and has have no filings.

We are told that Rachel takes size 3 in shoes, that Andrea's birthday is January 12, and that Paul's 'ears stick out but not enough to notice'.

On the other hand, information about disposition which would enable the reader to understand what sort of a person is being described is largely lacking. Adjectives like 'kind' and 'nice' recur, but it is unusual to find 'she is always cheerful. She is very playful and sometimes makes people laugh'. Reasons for friendship are seldom given, and where they are they are non-sequiturs.

> because I like Edward is that I allways play with him at playtime.
> I like Emma because she lives down the road.

Others are conventional if intense:

> I like Naleelee because she is very very very very kind and we play gams together.

Few children of this age speak about the relationship as distinct from the friend though Caroline says:

> If she had an accident I would cry a lot.

10–14-year-olds

From about ten onwards other features begin to appear. There is less listing of formal items, and individual characteristics, such as loyalty and understanding, are mentioned more. John commends the sensitivity of his friend

> for not calling when I was doing my home work.

However, there is less of this direct comment and more of a description of what the two do together, thus indicating that similarity of interests is one of the bases of friendship. Sometimes they are explicit about this. Stephen (13) says:

> An essential part of a friendship is that we both like doing the same things.
> I think one of my best friends is myself.

Similarity can even go as far as appearance:

> she is sort of my double, and we have the same hair styles.

There will be mutual liking, and reciprocity:

> someone who I can talk and listen to.

A friend should be helpful:

> When I work my friend's a mate
> He never does my homework late!

Girls particularly have a 'best friend' relationship which may well collapse:

> my best friend had decided to break up. I had to stand alone in the dinner queue.

Michaela (14) places great importance on the amount of affection remaining from her former 'best friend' as measured by presents:

> Unfortunately I was never her best friend again.
> But we did spend more on each other at Xmas than our other friends.

The intensity of close friendships amongst some girls approaches that of a love affair. Boys represent themselves as having more stable friendships.

It is not without significance that a proportion of the children do not designate human companions but a cat, a dog, a fishing rod, a snooker table, a pony, a 'pretend' friend of some years previously.

At this stage friendship is described rather than accounted for, often in terms of the things friends do together, but the influence of one friend on another is sometimes mentioned, as in this example by Keir (12):

> I knew he could be a bad influence on me but I always keep out of trouble

Only occcasionally, as in Stephen's piece, do we find *reflection* on aspects of friendship such as the individuality of the other.

> No matter how a friend is close, he is always different
> No matter what I think or I say a person has a mind of his own and a right to feel different. Perhaps this is a perfect friend?

14–17-year-olds

Writers in this age group are more likely to tend to *account for* a friendship, perhaps in terms of its history. Lorna (15.6) speaks of how Michelle first appeared as a stranger:

> When I would hear gossip about her she was often described as "You know, the weird-looking one" which in a sentence accurately described public opinion of her.

Growing knowledge of her, however, reveals a thoughtful individual very perceptive about other people. The gap between appearance and reality is brought out:

> One thing I have learnt from all this is that awkward appearances are no judge as what is on the interior . . . and no one should be denied the choice of a friendship because of the inviality (*sic*) of what they look like whether it is their coice or Mother Natures.

Suzanne (16) described a friend who moved from Eire at the same time she herself did, but whose history has been different. Rachel was unable to settle down, she did not 'come to terms with the move', idealised her early childhood, got mixed up with the wrong sort of people, and became depressed, 'dull and flat' instead of being 'lovely and bubbery'. There is a real attempt, not just to describe Rachel's present state, but to account for it in terms of her history.

Seila (15.8) distinguishes her relationship with Kim from one in which one is 'romantically involved', charting their childhood friends; and how she had to 'start afresh becoming friends again' in adolescence when 'the Kim I had known and had been close friends with no longer existed'.

With these writers individual dispositional characteristics are observed rather than the formal items mentioned by the younger children. Some of them generalise about friendship, and make perceptive comments on motive. Notice how Andrew (16) lists loyalty, self-interest, guilt, pity, as reasons for friendship.

> There are friends and there are friends, there is the one who stands by you at all times, or another who only wants to be friends cause you have a computer, snooker table, video etc. Then when your dad becomes redundant and you have to sell your things, they then desert and shun you. Some people befriend people out of guilt or just because they feel sorry for them.

Comment

Young children's descriptions of themselves and others are non-selective; they give 'social security' information, tell what they did, and occasionally speak of personal qualities of a general kind. There is no organising principle and information about the number of tooth-fillings lies alongside that on the number of brothers and sisters. The exception to this is when the composition is a list of likes or dislikes.

In the writings of the adolescents there is much more emphasis on personal qualities, particularly 'loyalty' and 'understanding'. There is a concern with relationships. Other writers try to account for relationships and people in terms of past as well as present; motives are perceived; the differences between the inner and outer person are commented on. Abstractions such as friendship can be discussed.

Adolescence presents the identity crises, and is notoriously associated with a re-emerged egotism. One would expect signs of this and of course they are present. But what is much more worthy of note under the circumstance is the degree of self-knowledge, the awareness of other people even the younger adolescents display. As John says:

Some people of may age believe the world revolves round them.

It could be argued that the very act of writing provides a quiet place in which the young people can pause and for a time, at least, see things in a different perspective.

8   What world is this?

Environment in literature

One thing the Crediton project considered was the relationship of human beings to their environment as expressed in writing. We are using the word 'environment' to mean non-human phenomena: that is, everything in the world except human beings. A helpful way of thinking of it would be as everything the specialist assistants are expected to supply for a film — from, for example, wheat fields in Russia, to food for a banquet, or the heroine's dresses: everything except the actors. Often descriptions of a writer's environment are confined to 'place': this is a much wider usage of the term.

People have always been interested in their environment, but in very different ways. For instance our present interest in natural landscape, the wilder and more unspoilt the better, which makes people seek holidays in the Lakes or the Scottish Highlands, only dates from Wordsworth and other romantic poets. Before that most people preferred a well-ordered man-made landscape; if it produced a good yield so much the better. Dr Johnson, looking at Glenshiel and its hills, commented: 'An eye accustomed to flowery pastures and waving harvests is astonished and repelled by this wide extent of hopeless sterility (quoted in Drabble, 1979, p. 124). Or take animals. Before the romantics, domestic animals in Britain were regarded very much as having to earn their keep as they are in many countries today, and not as pets. It was the romantics who introduced the present view of a domestic animal as a kind of superior human being. Some of them spoke, as St Francis had done, of animals as brothers and sisters. The poet Coleridge wrote verses 'To a Young Ass' (Coleridge, 1912, p. 74) with the line 'I hail thee *Brother* — spite of the fool's scorn'. Coleridge, who lacked a sense of the ridiculous, could never understand why he was satirised unmercifully for this by the Anti-Jacobins, who were the *Private Eye* of the time. He was true to his principles: his cottage was overrun with mice because he felt it cruel to set traps (Drabble, 1979, p. 167).

The environment that concerned the romantics was that of nature —

landscape and the flora and fauna in it. They felt themselves at one with nature. Wordsworth felt a 'presence' — a 'a motion and a spirit' —

> that impels
> All thinking things, all objects of all thought,
> And rolls through all things

But the 'objects of all thought' did not include towns and cities, offices and factories. Wordsworth 'in lonely rooms, and mid the din of towns and cities' longed for the 'sylvan Wye'. It was the nineteenth-century novelists, particularly Dickens, who legitimised them as a part of experience that had to be taken into account, not retreated from. A sentence from his description of Coketown in *Hard Times* (Chapter 5) will indicate the richness of his response even to an unpleasant scene:

> It had a black canal in it, and a river that ran purple with ill-smelling dye, and vast piles of buildings full of windows where there was a rattling and a trembling all day long, and where the piston of a steam engine worked monotonously up and down, like the head of an elephant in a state of melancholy madness.

The sense of place is seen by commentators as important in education. Inglis (1969, p. 22) placed its cultivation as one of the aims of English teaching — 'key images of place and home (of belonging, of roots, of community)' and Bennett (1985) speaks of it as one of the elements of cultural literacy. Certainly this is part of what we understand by 'environment' — but only part, for the environment may repel as well as comfort, and the former is as valid as the latter in human experience — it may be used to express not-belonging, rootlessness, no-community.

Again, environment as we use the term is not confined to 'place' or 'landscape' — it is any non-human fact or symbol which the writer may use to express his meaning. There are social environments created by the furnishing of rooms, the dress of people, the general speech and style. To quote Dickens again, this time *David Copperfield* (Chapter 4), Miss Murdstone's dress is part of the environment which he uses as a statement about her personality:

> It was Miss Murdstone who was arrived, and a gloomy looking lady she was . . . She brought with her two uncompromising hard black boxes with her initials on the lids in hard brass nails. When she paid the coachman she took her money out of a hard steel purse, and she kept the purse in a very jail of a bag which hung upon her arm by a heavy chain, and shut up like a bite. I had never, at that time, seen such a metallic lady altogether as Miss Murdstone was.

Some writers, such as Dickens, are fascinated by environment as such. But with any writer a sense of environment is bound to emerge without obvious description of it. In 'Jack and Jill' the scene is set by the well (implied), hill, pail of water, vinegar and brown paper. In 'Humpty Dumpty' the stage-set detail which creates great atmosphere is 'All the kings horses, and the kings men'. In 'Dilly Dilly' notice the sheer flavour created by 'Roses are red', 'lavender's blue', 'rosemary's green', 'sugar is sweet'. In 'Hickory Dickory Dock' notice how a detail from the environment takes a major role — the clock strikes one, which puts the mouse into retreat.

Perhaps we may best convey what we mean by the term 'environment' by two quotations. One is from Lewis Carroll (*Through the Looking-Glass*, Chapter 4), talking about the interest of various and apparently trivial things:

> The time has come', the Walrus said,
> 'To talk of many things:
> Of shoes — and ships — and sealing wax —
> of cabbages — and kings —

The other is from Louis Macneice ('Snow' in Larkin, 1973, p. 394) rejoicing in the sheer variety of things:

> World is crazier and more of it than we think,
> Incorrigibly plural. I peel and portion
> A tangerine and spit the pips and feel
> The drunkenness of things being various.

This, then is the background to our use of the term 'environment'. We shall now turn to look at work of writers aged seven to 18 and examine their use of environment.

My favourite place

7–12-year-olds
Children were asked to write on 'My Favourite Place'.

A group of seven-year-olds gave the minimum locational details such as the name of the place, and concentrated on an activity taking place there.

> My favourite place is when we go to the beach at Gorleston and we had a picnic   (Sharon, 7)

> My favourite place is Oulton Broad and in the place at Oulton Broad there is a swimming pool   (Mark, 7.6)

Other children of about this age, whilst still seeing activity as the important experience, nevertheless show themselves sensitive to sights, sounds, smells and tastes. Christine (8) says:

> I like going to the fun fare. I can smell candy floss and hamburgers they are lovely I like going on the helter skelter and the big wheel there is a knew thing it is called Pirat and it goes really high but it doesn't go over I like the rooer best of all when my mum go on it she Scream by my DaD like it.

The writers in this group do not contemplate, they act. The one who comes nearest to relating environmental details to his own sensations is Jerome:

> I like going on long walks because it is so peaceful and you can hear the birds and watch them. And you can sometimes see a fox. I like the smell of flowers My brother allways has to be carried. Once I saw some highland cattle. I allways see a lot of pheasants and pigeons and I sometimes zee a partridge Sometimes I have to climb very steep hills. I would like to come out at night. But I never have. And I also like to sail. I like the smell of the sea air. I like being outside in the country and by the sea.

Other children, aged between ten and 12 begin to try to account for their responses to a particular place. This is what Anna (10.9) has to say:

> The Favourite place I like is Kessingland wild life park because you can sometimes feed the animals and if you are hungry you can have a picnic or you can buy your food there and when you have finished your food you can have a look in the shops then you can see the wolf and when you throw him something he catches it and his den is very high. . . .

For Gemma the excitement of the 'favourite place' arises from her continuous involvement with it:

> First of all you come to a sort of tree house where you climb round the planks of wood to get to the house part then you have to walk the plank with a net underneath or you could just could walk along on another lot of round planks.

One group of compositions creates its effect by the cumulation of detail. In an account of Norwich Castle, for example, Clare (10.6) gives items indicating the environment, such as 'stuffed animals', 'bits of china', 'medals', 'lovely paintings', 'dungeons', 'lights off', 'dark', 'jail', 'well', 'drop pennies', 'metal bars', 'telescope', 'queen's crown', 'battlements'.

On the whole young children tended to write about family visits to places of interest or family outings of various kinds. But we also note in the work of 7–9-year-olds the child's personal room being a 'favourite place':

> I like my bedroom because it is private place for me and me only . . .! O It is drudefully messy its more like a rubish tip . . . But to my disopointment my mum has made it into an office ever since I have protested no luck so far BOO! I'll win don't you worry. . . .

12–18-year-olds

With the teenagers the appearance of a bedroom as a favourite place begins to emerge more strongly. In Bidwell's (1985) 13-year-old group of 32 nine wrote about this (of whom seven were girls — though of course this is not statistically significant). What is noticeable in several of these writings is that the environmental details are chosen in relation to the mood or attitude of the writer instead of being listed as with many of the younger children: Mary speaks of her bedroom matching her quiet mood, with its radio, armchair, magazine or book:

> When I am in a quite mood I want to lock myself away in seclusion. My bedroom fits this perfectly. I put my radio on and curl up in my armchair and browse through a magazine and read a book. . . .

Jenny also recognises the relationship of mood to environment:

> My moods tend to vary 'the place I like best'. If I feel down and tired and literally fed up with everything and everyone I feel the need to be alone somewhere, so that I don't take my mood out on someone unfortunate . . . I like to be alone in my room when the mood suits me. I feel as if I know the place, which I do, very well. I don't think I'd feel comfotable in a place that I didn't know, I'd feel lost and small.

Another feature is that many writers in their teens have considerable skill at detail. Take, for instance, Garth's landscape painting:

> Southern Argyule and its surrounding area has an atmosphere that is ancient and yet still lives. Forest floors covered ankle deep in pine needles that never change, stands on deserted hills, deserted crofts and forts . . .

Parry writes of Llanthany Abbey in Wales:

> It is best to be there on your own with the sun setting over the ridge of the black mountains as sheep baa and a buzzard whells over head . . . It is best on an April evening.

Some writers are moving towards symbolic use of environment. In Philip's piece his room has almost detached itself from the rest of the house as a statement of security:

> Because it is so high when it rains it felt like the room was separate from the rest of the house and it made you feel like curling up into a ball and going to sleep. The room is often as a strange place to be in as if there were spirits in the room. The room wanted to make you be on your own. It just made you feel at home.

A more developed use of symbolism occurs in this piece by Clair (15) where her own inner state of insecurity, apparently brought about by her parents' separation, is represented as not feeling at home. And the new state of affairs which has come about is represented by alien articles of furniture in the house:

> My home isn't my home, its where I live. When I come along the road I come to the same gate and the same path to the same front door and prick myself on the same holly bush. But it's not the same.
> It used to be the same till my Dad left. My Dad used to have a work bench in the garage but he took that.

He left all the furniture but when the settlement came through my Mum didn't like it and bought a new suite. I went along to choose it. It was cream with frills and deep upholstery. My Mum was very pleased with it but I thought it dominated the room, although I didn't say anything. I don't like sitting on it. The only place I feel at home is my bedroom because it had my old things there.

The following piece carries use of symbolism to a high degree of sophistication. It is deliberate, indeed the writer, Geoffrey (17), is highly conscious of his own skill, but this does not destroy its effectiveness. It seems to have the marks of a young writer's work in that it suggests the author is about a thousand years old, but the distancing can in fact be explained by its being from a draft for a novel.

Your room is your outward soul. When I first saw the room I was going to live in, with its dirty (not even consistently dirty) walls, and its chipped paintwork, and the indecipherable carpet, I felt it was a dreary soul for any one to have inhabited. Though the dirty windows when the sun penetrated it showed up myriads of spots of dust, like myriads of little sins, and worst of all someone else's sins.
The landlord wouldn't improve it, but he didn't mind if I did. I painted everything white, and the floor black, hid the carpet in the cupboard, and placed a single circular rush mat in the centre of the floor. The whole effect wasn't so much bare as austere. I though it suited me well; that was my austere period. There were still spots of dust in the sunlight, even if fewer. But they were mine. My own sins were much more acceptable than other people's.

Environment in narrative

The writings we have examined so far have come from a direct request for a response to the environment, in this case a favourite place. Consequently environmental details may have a more prominent place than in other forms of writing such as narrative. In this section we shall look at the response to environment in narratives.

It has been suggested (Wilkinson *et al.*, 1980) that we may regard simple narrative as having two main elements — the *core* of the narrative on the one hand, the simple relation of events; and the *elaborations* of the narrative on the other (the term is from Kernan, 1977). The elaborations may be of two kinds — comments on the events, on the one hand ('This proved an extremely foolish thing to do'), and details to enrich the interest (background, descriptions, and so on). Clearly this last is one of the functions environment will serve.

For reasons connected with the number of things to be done at once, young writers tend to give only the core narrative.

3.1 5–11-year-olds
Let us look at the way in which younger children differ from older in the writing of a (previously told) story about a dragon. Lorraine is aged six. Hers is bare narrative:

> the dragon breath the whole place up then there was nothing to be see

But Michelle supplies a setting:

> Once there was a dragon
> He lived in Mexico in a hole

And Lee and incidental comment:

> Once upon a time there was a dragon who lived in a cave. He liked breathe fire. He was a nasty dragon. he didn't like people so they put him in jail . . .

Laura goes further. On the one hand she gives information about the girl's state of mind; on the other, environmental information about place.

> Once upon a time there was a dragon who lived under the sea. One day when the dragon was under the sea bathing he heard some footsteps. it was a little girl. She was coming to bath. She didn't know the dragon was there, and the then the dragon saw the little girl and the little girl saw the dragon and the little girl was very frightened so she ran away and the dragon said to not run away Im a friend of your and they played together.

In the work of 9–10-year-olds in contrast we may look at the elaborations. In response to a similar story Shaun writes:

> The two Dragons who did not like each other
>
> One night it was cler and stary moonlight night, in china there was muddy field and a dragon was flying overhead until it saw another dragon in his favourite spot. . . .

A boy in the 10–11-year-old group, Peter, makes full use of the two types of elaboration — explanation and environmental detail. The core narrative is simple: the people come to see the dragon. All the rest is explanation and description, particular about the behaviour of the crowd, and the nature of the armed force.

The Chinese Dragon

Core narrative	Elaboration I (Explanation, etc.)	Elaboration II (Environment)
The new year had started		People were everywhere. There were clowns but

the thing everyone
had come to see was
the Chinese dragon

The crowds were
cheering for the
chinese dragon.

People screamed
when they sore the
dragon

It wasn't like it
should be it was all
green it didnt have
eight leg it had four

People were
running over over
people

The dragon killed
half of them with
one blow

People heard the
sirens of the police
car

One of the police-
men radioed the
force

In a matter of
minutes planes and
armed cars came
with some guns

One of the guns
fired hundred
rounds a minute

Guns fired

and hit directly be-
tween the eyes and

he fell to the ground

3.2 11–18-year-olds

Writers in their early teens are more likely to be able to establish a scene
effectively and economically. In the following pieces writers are responding to a picture of two little children behind a wire fence:

It was cold and dark and gloomy. What were they doing there. They were
imprisoned . . .

(Moira, 12)

In the wire cage the children wondered what had happened when John
walked into the case and gazed out to see only a grey brick wall and on top

of that there was a load of spickes and barbed wire so it was no use trying
to escape

(Hanna, 11.6)

Over the next three months, and indeed years, I never forgot this one scene.
The beds were just blanket, one for a pillow and one as mattress, sheets and
blanket, all rolled in to one.

(Kenneth, 12.7)

Hedda (12.2) goes further and in her work the environment is beginning to function as symbolic of a world of freedom. And incidentally she
tries to be accurate about the children, their speech and their clothes.

Through the wire

What can you see, Michael? asked Jeremy.

I'm looking at them lovely trees, I wanna live in one' replied Michael.

Jeremy and Michael had lived in a camp all their lives so far and still
probably live in one until they die. The clothes that they were given to wear
were either too small or too big.

Michael is now five and Jeremy six. Their mother's and father's have to
work all day long with Jeremy's brother Mat who is nine. Jeremy and
Michael are nearly always standing at the wire looking at the countryside
they will never be able to wander in.

'You know that hut thing over there I think it is beautiful do you? wondered Michael.

'Yeah, but I like the place of grass better', answered Jeremy.

Features of environment occur in the narrative much as we noticed in
the composition on 'My Favourite Place'. The most notable development
is from literal to metaphorical. With some writers environment ceases to
be merely background, however picturesque, and becomes part of the
statement. In the picture of the two little children behind a wire fence the
obvious symbol is one of imprisonment, and a fair proportion of teenage
writers make use of this. The work of Terry (16) is clearly much influenced by space fiction, but he uses the conventions to bring out most
effectively the equation of prison and life:

One day my brother escaped, but he came back very soon.

Why have you come back, I asked.

'Because there's no where to go', he said, looking fearful.

How do you mean, I said, 'What's over the hill', I asked.

'Nothing' he said. 'The top of that hill is the edge of a cliff'.

I began to understand. 'You mean we're on an island. There's water all
round', I said.

'No, nothing'.

'You mean there's outer space', I joked.

'No, he said, breaking down, 'there's nothing'.

He recovered a little. 'You'd better believe it Hank', he said.

'This is all there is this prison, there's nothing else' . . .

The equation is made quite explicitly in Gavin's writing: 'This is what life is . . .' The environment and its features have in fact become the central fact, making the central statement: they are not incidental. Gavin (17) draws particular attention to the condition of the yard and the factory, and repeats this in the last paragraph. The relationship of people to environment is movingly brought out: 'childhood behind a fence' could be the title to the piece.

> It had never been any different. As far as I could remember it had always been like this. It had always been a squalid yard, muddy when it was wet, dusty when it was dry. But most of all, looking on back on my childhood what I remember was the boredom. There was nothing to do. There was nothing to play with except a few stones and broken bits of concrete. So all the time my brother and I did nothing. We just stood at the fence and looked out into the street outside. Outside I can remember there was a decayed factory made of corrugated iron, with broken windows . . .
>
> It never will be any different. This is what life is a squalid yard, muddy when it is wet, dusty when it is dry. But most all the boredom. There is nothing to do. The factory outside has rotted even more than ten years ago. But even if there were work what could I do? What does your childhood behind a fence equip you for? Anyway who wants to work anyway?

Comment

There is, it appears, a general developmental sequence in the way that young writers use the environment. At first there is no environmental reference because the writer has enough to cope with in making simple uncontextualised statements. The next step may be the introduction of not particularly relevant environmental detail. In the bed-to-bed composition which is so frequent, details of food eaten, TV programmes watched, may be offered gratuitously. The environmental items begin to be introduced as the meaning requires, the writer becoming more aware of the reader's needs. Growing confidence may cause specific scene painting, sometimes because words begin to intoxicate. What seems to distinguish adolescent writing from that preceding it is the ability to symbolise, to require features of environment to carry meaning, not just to provide a setting for it.

> My home isn't my home, it's where I live.

9 The disruption of the probable

1. Narrative as a primary act

In a famous phrase Hardy (1968) speaks of narrative as a primary act of mind:

> My argument is that narrative . . . is not to be regarded as an aesthetic invention used by artists to control, manipulate and order experience, but as a primary act of mind transferred to art from life . . . we dream in narrative, day dream in narrative, remember, anticipate, hope, despair, believe, doubt, plan, revise, criticise, construct, gossip, learn, hate and love by narrative. In order really to live we make up stories about ourselves and others, about the personal as well as the social past and future. (Hardy, in Meek et al., 1977, p. 12–13).

Narrative as a primary act of mind seems a powerful proposition. Yet it is not a primary act of mind if it is preceded, as it must be, by acts of labelling of people, objects, actions; or by a classificatory act of mind such as produces concepts, plurals and superordinates. The point is that there are other acts of mind open to human beings from early days. Narrative nevertheless is, and must be, a very important one because we carry out actions in a temporal world. It is a form of coherent ordering in which young children engage, and to which they are exposed in the storying around them.

Under these circumstances we would expect much early writing in schools to be in narrative form. And this writing can be in a very real sense the story of the children's lives, an essential feature of, and means in their personal development. This was one of the main concerns of the original Crediton work; the other was for far wider criteria of evaluation than are currently in use, reflecting such development. Both these concerns lie behind the research described in this chapter. The purpose of the research was to describe the features of children's narrative writing between the ages of seven and 13.

2. Research design

The design of this research (implemented following a small pilot study) was to present the same three tasks, all intended to elicit narrative prose,

99

to three groups of children, aged approximately seven, ten and 13 years. Three neighbouring schools on the outskirts of Norwich, England, kindly cooperated — an all-ability high school, one of its feeder middle schools and, in turn, its feeder first school. Thus the groups were likely to be similar in terms of key variables. Writing was elicited from one class in each age group, by class teachers working with their own pupils, after detailed discussion with the researcher.

Three narrative tasks were set, in a prescribed order.
1. An autobiographical narrative, an account of something memorable because it made the writer happy, or sad, or was in some other way interesting.
2. An imaginative narrative, in response to one of a choice of three pictures as a stimulus.
3. An imaginative narrative intended for an audience of, say five years old.

As many decisions as possible were left open to the writers, regarding the selection and shaping of ideas — for instance there were no prescribed titles, or required length — and teacher support was sufficient to maintain the task, without teacher intervention to shape ideas.

The 240 scripts thus collected were read and reread many times in the process of analysing them in terms of the descriptive models detailed below.

3. Models of analysis

Models of analysis began to evolve from close interaction between theory and first-hand data. Attempts to produce a composite, graded description of increasingly well-formed narratives were discarded, on the grounds that they attempted to conflate developments belonging on different dimensions. A number of models were clearly needed, and the Crediton models were used with appropriate modification which it is unnecessary to detail here. It is sufficient to say that they — particularly the affective — were making significant discriminations in development across the age range covered.

The contribution of this present research is felt to lie in the formulation of a new model, the 'Development of Storying', associated with the description of temporal, spatial and eventual probabilities.

The development of storying

The storying model seeks to represent the movement from the simple narrative as a temporally sequenced account of ordinary events to the more elaborate and effective narrative that includes the occurrence of something out of the ordinary, with all that that entails. It rests on two concepts, that of 'ordinariness' and that of the 'disturbance of probabilities'.

The concept of ordinariness

When coping with the heavy cognitive and physical demands of the writing process, young children tend to draw upon very familiar everyday experiences for content. Nothing disturbs the ordinariness of the daily pattern, and bedtime is the obvious conclusion to the chronological narrative, there being no tension to resolve. The overriding impression gained from reading numerous such texts is that they are highly predictable. In storying terms, the ordinariness and predictability of definition is proposed as follows: The events of narrative are ordinary when they conform to all expectations of time, place and social relationships. Events occur in time, in a location where the laws of nature pertain, and people and objects are assigned their expected roles and uses. Thus in the light of the reader's knowledge of the world, rather than through literary devices, the narrative is seen as *predictable*. Furthermore, this ordinariness renders the events potentially *repeatable* on any number of subsequent occasions. Such predictable, repeatable events are related in strict chronological sequence.

With reference to chronology, it is of course a basic requirement of narrative that at least two clauses should be temporally ordered in relation to each other (Labov and Waletsky, 1967). Thus the sentence 'I shot and killed him' fulfils the requirement of narrative, whereas 'I laughed and laughed' does not. Young children are accustomed to being asked to order events, such as what they did at school, or what they did at the weekend, or to sequence their way through key points in the day, such as breakfast time, school time and play time. It does not seem unreasonable to expect that children of seven to eight should have the ability to relate events in temporal sequence.

The label of 'chronicle' is posited for that writing which combines such characteristics of ordinariness and chronology, and represents the baseline from which storying develops.

'Chronicle' is not here intended to be derogatory, a 'mere' chronicle. Rather it is a simple statement of a stage that encompasses the characteristics already outlined, and in addition implies a lack of selectivity of detail. Scholes and Kellogg (1966) mention such a lack in respect of historical narratives, or chronicles, and it is similarly implied in the *Concise Oxford Dictionary*'s definition of chronicle as '*a continuous* register of events in order of time'. This lack of selectivity serves to emphasise the essential ordinariness of events, where nothing is allowed to assume greater importance.

This type of narrative does not necessarily correlate with brevity or poor mechanical skill. Some texts of considerable length are neatly produced, and incorporate increasing detail. Nevertheless, they still fail to move beyond the bounds of chronicle.

The special occasion

A small shift away from ordinariness, though by no means a proven necessary stage, appears in some children's work, identified as a 'special occasion narrative'. Entirely as the result of free choice, not teacher direction, a narrative may be set on a fixed date, such as Christmas Day or Mothering Sunday. This seems to represent an attempt to move beyond ordinariness, yet further examination of such texts suggests that this has not been achieved. This is explained in terms of the shared cultural expectations of the writer and the reader. Given certain expectations of events the text proves entirely predictable and the events potentially repeatable in subsequent years. The probabilities suffer no disruption.

The disruption of probabilities

Disruption of the probable pattern immediately renders events less predictable and less repeatable. The unusual event or behaviour, the socially unacceptable behaviour or unfortunate accident that disturbs the probabilities entails in itself some further response and resolution. It leaves the reader wondering what will happen next, with a genuine curiosity. The capacity thus to arouse the reader is precisely what constitutes E. M. Forster's definition of a 'story' in his literary work on *Aspects of the Novel* (1927). The child who writes thus is producing stories not chronicles. They may be brief pieces, written with obvious mechanical difficulty, but they are stories. Some texts may be comparatively lengthy, with a good deal of chronicle of ordinariness surrounding the main disturbance. Only slowly does selectivity develop, leaving the influence of chronicle completely behind.

The model seeks to indicate the major types of disruption of probabilities that occur regularly in early stories. They may range from slight deviations from the norm to considerably more bizarre deviations, with a tendency towards the violent act or accident.

Whilst early stories hinge on one description of probabilities, later stories may contain two or more discrete events, each with its own disturbance of probability. The relationship between events is temporal rather than causal, and usually involving the same characters. It is interesting to speculate as to why this occurs. Given cognitive limitations on planning a unified whole, the writer may respond to the exhortation to write 'more' or to make it 'more exciting' by adding on extra incidents.

The yet more fully developed story would seem to revert to the use of one major disruption of the probable pattern, with the surrounding detail being increasingly relevant to the narrative. Furthermore, the disturbance of probability is no longer introduced only at the point of occurrence, but is foreshadowed, pervading the text almost from the beginning. Choice of word, phrase, and detail are significant, the curiosity of readers is *quickly* aroused and their attention held as tension mounts. With the increasing range of devices available, the writer maximises the storytelling, allowing nothing to remain commonplace. Time, place, weather, the creeping, dashing, whispering or screaming characters are all significant.

At the highest level of storying proposed here, the reasons, intentions and motives of characters are made explicit; cause and effect can be traced; the story reveals not only what happened but why. In E. M. Forster's literary terms this latter point would be the element that turns 'story' into plot. The writer may make 'more' out of 'less', or at least out of fewer incidents, as an interest in people develops.

The story written at this level is a cohesive, effective whole. The reader, on reaching the end, is prompted to reflect back over the structure as a whole, and may perceive more in it than its constituent events. The narrative may indeed have been used, as C. S. Lewis suggests, as the net to capture what cannot be sequenced (Lewis, 1977).

Range of disturbances
(a) Unusual overt behaviour/activity — e.g., he ran away (*so* his Mum and Dad called the police.); he wouldn't eat his breakfast (*so* his mother was displeased); unusual visits, outings, housemoving etc. in autobiography.
(b) Unacceptable overt behaviour, of one or more persons as measured against social norms — e.g, deliberate aggression, robbery, kidnapping, provoking a response from others.
(c) Conflict on wider scale — Germany, Vietnam, Falklands — provoking loss, separation, eventual resolution.
(d) Accidental occurrences — after ordinary beginnings — getting lost while out walking; wide range of accidental injuries and breakages in autobiography.
(e) Involuntarily behaviour — disturbs daily pattern — e.g. through illness — 'my nanny couldn't get her breath', etc.
(f) New element introduced into familiar setting — requires explanation or revelation.
(g) Some or all laws of nature are disrupted — signalling 'story' e.g. of fairy-tale type. May include — imaginative time, past or future; anthropomorphism; normal children stumbling into 'another world' via caves, tunnels, dreams; witches, wizards, fairies, elves, goblins with supernatural powers. At early story stage, such a disruption of the setting seems to be the 'story signal'.

A model of storying

ST 1   *Chronicle*
ST 1.1   *Pre-chronicle.* Aggregate of action and stasis statements, with minimal temporal or causal relationships.
ST 1.2   *Chronicle.* Relation, in order of time, of events that are ordinary, predictable, potentially repeatable. Lack of selectivity of events and details. Typically events occur within one day ending with bed. Occurs in autobiographical and imaginative narrative.
ST 1.3   *Elaborated chronicle.* Bearing all features of chronicle, but with increased elaboration of setting, actual speech of characters may be given, more detail of events. Occurs in autobiographical and imaginative narrative.
ST 1.4   *Chronicle of special occasion.* Writer freely chooses to relate, in order of time, events on a specified occasion, e.g., Mother's Day. No disturbance of probability, given shared cultural expectations between writer and reader. Occurs in autobiography and imaginative narrative.
ST 2   *Story*
ST 2.1   *Simple Story.* Relation of events in temporal sequence, little elaboration of core events. One overt disturbance of probabilities, entailing response and resolution. Disturbance introduced only at point of occurrence. May be starkly realised or surrounded by some chronicle. Selectivity increases slowly. Degree of disruption varies, outcomes (e.g., punishment) often disproportionate. Occurs in autobiography and fiction.
ST 2.2   *Story with additions.* Relation in temporal sequence of two or more events, each containing disturbance of probability. Links between events are temporal. Lack of logical unity leaves ending unsatisfying, as it becomes a chronicle of the end of the day and so to bed. Disturbances introduced only at point of occurrence. Range of disturbance as in (a) – (g) above (see p. 104).
Occurs frequently in imaginative narrative.
In autobiography, recall in temporal sequence of a number of memorable but unrelated incidents.
ST 2.3   *Developed story.* Narration of sequence of events where one major disturbance of probability is the focus, entailing what follows.
Writer begins to make more out of fewer incidents by increase in elaborate detail, some selected, some still superfluous.
By foreshadowing the disruption early in the narrative, arousing reader's curiosity about events. Time, place, speech begin to have narrative significance – e.g. '*very early* in the morning'; 'a ghostly wood'; 'Mummy said Don't go too far'.
Range of disturbance similar to (a) – (g) (see p. 104), but disturbance

and outcome more fully realised. Outcomes are wider range, the home–lost–found–home-again pattern begins to be broken. In autobiography, disturbance is alluded to and more fully realised. In addition to memorable accidents, there are records of successful achievements.

ST 2.4   *Well-developed story*. Displays developments on many dimensions, resulting in a unified story, with relevant elaborations of events, characters, settings. Disturbances of probabilities occurs from range given. Additionally, especially in autobiography the uniqueness of a situation is what renders it unpredictable and unrepeatable in identical form — 'the first time I ever . . .'

Disturbance pervades text from beginning. Time, place, weather, personal characteristics all significant. Verbs of common occurrence are inadequate for people who 'rush', 'dash', 'whisper', 'scream'. Excitement, suspense, or surprise may be present, to hold reader's attention through to resolution. Ending may not be safe 'happily-ever-after' type, but may include disappearance, or even death etc.

Awareness of genre-models in some narratives — the crime story, the adventure tale, fairy tale, moral or explanatory tale. The whole is more than the sum of its parts. Reader can reflect upon a cohesive whole, which may have captured an abstract notion — e.g., loneliness; fear; anxiety conquered; achievement; courage; poverty; friendship; happiness; a sense of justice.

Storying in children's writing

In order to illustrate the application of the model we turn to examples from the children's scripts.

Seven-year-olds
In autobiography, the task set was intended to give the pupils the scope to go beyond the level of chronicling daily events (which style is the inevitable result of a regular demand for 'news'). Relatively few of the texts are rated at the level of simple chronicle (ST 1.2) from this assignment.

One text which is thus rated is by Wayne (7.10). It might be given the gloss of 'having a friend to play', an ordinary and repeatable occurrence in the lives of most young children. He records:

> Richard came round and we had a game of space invaders and I got 1000 points and then we had a game of marbles for 15 minutes and then Richard went home.

The piece is shaped by entering the time sequence at the point of Richard's arrival, and making an exit from it with his departure. Details about Richard are singularly lacking, though the reader assumes that he is a friend of Wayne's. This text would be regarded as within the ST 1.2 stage, as are two other straightforward scripts.

A small shift is seen in narratives set on a named occasion, where the writer strives to record a memorable occurrence, yet all the incidents remain normal within the cultural expectations of the reader. This was noted in narratives such as this one by Claire (7.10):

> Yesterday it was Mothers day and I bought a box of chocolate and my brother bought some hairspray, and my sister bought some cream to put on her face. and . . .

This and a number of other scripts from this age group were classified at the ST 1.4 level of a chronicle of a special occasion, which lacked any overt evaluation of the significance of the occasion.

At the level of ST 2.1., (a simple story containing one disturbance of probabilities) there were a number of texts by seven-year-olds. As the model suggests, some such stories embed the disturbance in a chronicle of the more ordinary events of the day, while others deal more directly with the unusual occurrence. A fortuitous illustration presented itself in the data, when two children wrote of the same incident, in which they were both involved, but wrote in differing ways. Claire's account chronicles events preceding the disturbance.

> Yesterday me and Sarah went round for Matthew, James S——'s little brother . . .

After describing in some detail the outing and return of Matthew in his pushchair, Claire describes seeing something:

> I saw a yellow and green thing in a dack (?) and I walked back I saw it was a toad I called Sarah and when I told her she nearly jumped out of her skin.

The reader's curiosity mounts during this. What will happen, next?

> Sarah went to tell the boys, and when they came Sarahs brother Martin He kept touching it with his glove and me and Sarah kept screeming and a man came out and put it in his garden.

This represents a story, not a chronicle, and contains some detail. Compare this with Martin's briefer account, rendered in full. The impact is slightly lessened by now knowing the situation, but his story is effective in arousing the reader's curiosity:

> On Sunday I was playing whit Martin Q—— at a game of cricket and me and Martin had 200 runs and suddenly my sister came up and she said was yelling and she said Theres a toad so we all follerd her and when we got there Martin touched it and then it started jumping and Claire and Sarah started screming and then this man spoylt it all becaus Martin got it on the road and then he said it came from his garden so he tok it in and we went in for lunch and then me and Martin had a game of soldgers.

This represents an effective simple story at the ST 2.1 level, based on the disturbance to the pattern of the day brought about by finding the toad, which provoked the touching and screaming; and led to the man ending the situation by returning the toad to his garden.

So runs the main trend of storying in the seven-year-olds' autobiography, though one writer, despite enormous problems with spelling and punctuation, produced a text verging on ST 2.2 level, a story with an additional incident, temporally related to the first, added on at the end.

It is a measure of the difficulty experienced by the youngest writers in responding to the pictures for the imaginative narrative task that just under half the class managed to sustain a narrative response. The others, when faced with pictures which had of necessity to be suitably mature for thirteen-year-olds, found the cognitive load heavy, and resorted to naming or labelling the people in the pictures, and elements from the background. However, amongst those who sustained a narrative, there were examples of simple chronicle, special occasion narrative, and simple story level.

In contrast, many children achieved a level of storying equal to the ST 2.1 story in their third assignment, the narrative intended for small children. In this task they felt more comfortable, more secure, and wrote — not with a struggle — but with the confidence borne of having a clear model for story in mind. Thus witches, wizards, fairies and anthropomorphism are all found. Arguably the most successfully developed story produced in this assignment was penned by a writer who struggled unsuccessfully to sustain a narrative in response to the picture. The story deals directly with the disturbance of probabilities, in the appearance of the witch, which entails all that follows in this satisfyingly complete, and for this age group complex, account:

The Witch and Me

> One day I went for a walk in the woods. Suddenly I hear this funny laughing in the distance then I saw a witch up on her broomstick suddenly I was up on her broomstick as well and I flue to her case it was on the other side of the Misty Mountains I was frighten suddenly she cast a spell on me I was running to the entrance but it was closed just as the spell was going to hit me I jumped behind a rock the spell bounced on the rock and hit the witch she turned into a frog then I got up and took the broomstick and looked at the buttons and swichs near the door I prested one of the swichs it opened the door I flue back home I told my mum but she did not believe it.
> The End

Ten-year-olds
Characteristic of the ten-year-old's autobiographical narratives is the disappearance of the simple chronicle, and the much firmer establishment of the ability to tell a simple story. Indeed, half the sample of

scripts in this age group fall into the stage of simple storying, where one particular disturbance of probabilities entails what follows (ST 2.1). A large number of the stories relate to accidents (breakages, falls from bicycles and so on), illnesses, or mischievous behaviour. This is also true of the nature of the disturbances where a number of memorable but otherwise unconnected incidents are recalled, in a number of stories rated at the ST 2.2 level. Typical of such stories is that of Justin (9.9), one of the younger pupils in this class:

When I was small about three I was wondering about the house, I was wondering about for three hours then I walked into the kitchen where my mum was doing the ironing and then she went out of the room I triped over the wire and the iron was still hot and it fell on me. I was in hospital for 3 days. Two weeks ago I was playing football and I skided on the mud and cut the side of my leg. In my back garden I was playing football and when I was trying a penaltey at my dad and it broke two things a window and behind it was a mirror and that broke two. so then I had quite a bid of bad luck.

Typical of the storying at this level is the rather fuller realisation of the first incident, followed by more sketchy coverage of successive ones.

Narratives which seem to be working towards the ST 2.3 level of a developed story (and there were three in the sample class) all centre around one incident, with elements of both semantic and expressive elaboration for the reader, foreshadowing of the events to come, and some evaluation in the text, if even only to a modest degree. Thus a boy who scored the winning goal in an important football match says 'I will never forget that day', while the girl hurt in a fall from a pony descibed it as 'one of the most terrifying things that has happened to me'.

One type of storying which does not disappear from the autobiographical writing of the ten-year-olds is that of the chronicle of special occasion. Though simple chronicles cease, a number of writers describe in considerable detail the chronological sequence of events on an 'occasion', though nothing untoward transpires. Whilst the reader may guess that the occasion was important to the writer, there is no textual evidence of the significance or evaluation of the event. Carol (10.4) chronicles her arrival at a gymnastics club display in just such a fashion, from the time of arrival, through lining up in the corridor, going into the hall and giving the display, to coming home to fish and chips.

In imaginative narratives in this age group the ability confidently to tell a simple story again seems well established in the majority, with some pupils offering stories with additions, and a few showing evidence of working towards the ST 2.3 level of a well-developed story.

Among stories for small children, too, there are texts at the level of simple stories, stories with two complete incidents temporally ordered, and two or three well-developed stories, representing a considerable achievement in detailed storying, with appropriate explanations and settings for the audience.

13-year-olds

The greatest number of narratives, both personal and imaginative, at this age, cluster around the ST 2.3 level of a developed story. Some writers are striving to achieve this, many operate comfortably within this stage, while a few appear to be thrusting beyond it to a fully developed story level (ST 2.4).

In personal narratives, special occasions are explicitly evaluated in the text, for example, 'a trip I will never forget'; 'exhausting but still enjoyable' and so on. Narratives centring on a disturbance of probability include a high degree of elaboration and foreshadowing to heighten the story for the reader, and the emotions associated with an incident become a key feature of those accounts that strive towards the ST 2.4 level of storying. Two examples may be given.

Lynda (13.3) relates to the tale of a holiday excursion. She includes detail for her reader and disturbance pervades her text, with a sense of the calm before the storm:

> Visiting Gozo, the sister island to Malta and Comino might seem pretty boring. Just the normal routine, get on the boat, cross the sea, get off the boat, look around, then come home. That's what I thought until I actually tried it out. We caught the ferry and the journey over the sea was calm and the sky was blue. We crossed with not a care in the world . . .

The setting is firmly established, and it is equally clear that the trip is not going to match up to the expectations stated at the beginning. At first, on arrival on Gozo, the visit seems to take the pattern of a tourist trip, again with some details given. During a meal in a café it begins to rain. The seriousness of the situation is indicated not by a succession of adjectives about the weather, but by the action of the café proprietor:

> my sister went to the toilet and she found the cloakroom was half full of rainwater. She told the café owner, who immediately grabbed his money and his bottle of whisky and left . . .

The moves of the family and others, from building to building in search of refuge from the flood waters, are carefully detailed (in fact a sketch map is supplied — the only illustration drawn by any pupil in any of the assignments). After spending the night on the island, the family return to Malta next day by chartered fishing boat to find similar scenes of devastation there. The writer operates very comfortably within the ST 2.3 level of storying, with an undoubtedly dramatic tale to tell.

Less dramatic in themselves are the narrative events of Peter's scripts. He travels by van from Norwich to Thetford with fellow members of a brass band to play in a competition. On arrival they have to unload their instruments and music stands, set up on stage, and play their set pieces. The disturbance of the normal pattern comes from the fact that Peter has never played in a competition before, and the impact of the piece comes from the realisation in the text of his feelings on such an occasion.

> Many of my friends had already been to contests and were not worrying, but to be quite honest I was very nervous.

His satisfaction comes from concentrating hard, determined not to 'muck things up', rather than from the placing of the band in the contest, which is not in fact revealed. At the end his relief is clear:

> We done well. 'My God' I said to myself, 'I'm damn glad thats over!'

There is a high degree of awareness of emotion and evaluation of the significance of the situation to the writer at the time. Thus it becomes a story at two levels, the story of events, and the story of emotions, and is working towards ST 2.4 level.

The picture stimuli offered this age group a challenge which both daunted and yet intrigued them. They offered sustained narrative responses, of the ST 2.3 and ST 2.4 levels, centred around accidents, murder on religious grounds, bereavement, and political struggles, to name but a few disruptions of ordinariness. Again concern with emotion assumes greater importance than in the texts of younger writers; and it is this which raises the storying to two levels — the narrative of events carrying with it a narrative of human emotions. An illustration of this is to be found in a story by James, prompted by a picture of a young girl and a ventriloquist's dummy. An annual junior talent competition serves as the setting for the narrative of events relating to the contest, but it is also the story of the girl's eventual mastery over her own emotions, ending thus:

> It was good . . . but not good enough a little boy had walked off with the prize but she didn't mind, at least she knew she had the courage to go on stage and perform.

In response to the same picture Claire G. tells a narrative of events when an old man dies, and his daughter, son-in-law and granddaughter clear out the loft afterwards. Yet the story also represents the granddaughter's coming to terms with some of her emotions, and concludes:

> That night Diane sat Charlie (the puppet) on the windowsill. Just think my grandad made you. Diane thought to herself. 'I'll keep you for ever and ever! Thank you Grandad for making puppets!!!'

The writers themselves are perhaps seeking to understand some of the complexities of the human condition, through their narratives.

The pressures of the human condition on a wider scale pervade some stories in this age group. For David K. (13.) the political struggle in

Poland provides a setting. The actions of one particular rioter in a crowd represent the disturbance of probabilities, entailing what follows for him, and for his family. The completion of his story is brought about by a reunion of the family in jail, though the wider issues remain unresolved in the story, as in life. The stimulus picture for this narrative is clearly that of the family behind a barred window, and it is tempting to infer that the writer sees in it some degree of symbolism for the repression of a nation. Certainly the opening of the narrative encourages the reader to take this wider view, before concentrating on the concrete details of the family in the incidents. The story begins:

> It was Poland, the winder of discontent 1981. Martial law had been imposed, Lech Wowensa had been put under house arrest by General Yaraselski and his fellow millitary leaders. Times moved on — it was now May the next year, the people were getting restless. Solidarity, the working people's union was working underground. Then the feelings that had been bottled up inside their selves were let loose.

Storying at this level represents ST 2.4 a level that caters for the reader with an elaborated, heightened story, that arouses curiosity and promotes thinking in the reader.

In writing imaginative narratives for young children these pupils seemed able to draw on models of 'story', and to consider 'the story form' as an object. Many texts showed the influence of fairy-tale and folklore, where wicked witches receive their just desserts, where abducted princesses are rescued and married by worthy young men. One story, clearly derived from the Little Engine stories of Rev. Awdry, features the modest engine victorious over the large, ostentatious engine. Anthropomorphic tales of mice, hamsters, and a Super Bunny, space stories and three involving 'ordinary people' complete the range.

At a straightforward level of storying with considerable detail Rachel portrays an unhappy girl, Amanda, whose happiness is secured when she is allowed to keep a small puppy. Other stories contain indications of storying at levels, the literal and the symbolic. Again there may be a danger of reading out something that the writer did not intend. However, it seems possible that these writers, using as models folk tales where good and evil, strength and weakness are clearly symbolised, have found that the form lends itself to symbolism of their own. Presented with the opportunity of writing in this form, for a young audience (thereby removing some of the pressures of adult judgement) a number of writers seem to approach the symbolic level.

Carol's narrative uses a familiar children's story theme of the toys in the toy cupboard coming alive at night. The narrative of events contains a developed story in itself, in which the traditional toys sabotage the new-fangled space-age toys by removing cogs, springs and batteries, so that the children will return to their old favourites. At another level an interpretation could be proposed in terms of new versus old ideas, or in terms of protest against the increasing armaments of the modern world, represented in the story by the 'anti-stuffed toy missiles' possessed by the space-age toys.

Similar concern regarding the nuclear threat is blatantly symbolised in Graeme's text. In a sense, this writer has constructed a modern fairy-tale (tinged with political satire) of the sort that perhaps he would like to be able to believe in. He uses the form of the story of banishment of the evil one and restoration of peace and happiness, as a vehicle for his modern concerns. Suitability for his audience has become less of a concern than the desire to shape meaning for himself. His story is quoted at length:

Bad Mr Nuke Gets his Just Reward

In a land many miles away a wicked man has his home in an un-used flat. He was banished there a few years ago. His name is Nuclear Missile, but people call him Mr. Nuke. He lives along in exile now, but not all that many nights ago he lived here in Peaceland.

Then, nobody was safe. Before he came we lived a nice peaceful life, with no crimes and wars, in tranquility. But along came Mr. Nuke. He came with a spear and robbed us. Anyone who tried to stop him ended up spear-red to death. Next he crossed the seven seas and killed us with swords. Few survived. One month later he attached us with clubs. Soon he dropped bombs on us.

Then we decided enough is enough. We formed C.N.D. MOST SAID .n.d. stood for Campaign for Nuke's Detention, but I think it stood for Campaign for Nuclear Disarmament, for if we disarmed him he couldn't kill us. anyway, we took partitions, hundreds signed them, to the Government. They Didn't help.

We knew he'd come back soon. Come back he did, but we were ready for him. As he charged down the streets of Peacetime, the biggest town in Peaceland, we through a net over him. We'd got him at last. We flew over the seas and dropped him off . . .

From then until today we've been ruled by the S.D.P. or the Safely Defended Party. Peaceland has returned to being peaceful, Peacetime has recovered from Mr. Nuke and we're all happy.

In terms of its attempt to capture more than a sequence of events this text shows the writer striving for the ST 2.4 level of storying, and represents an important illustration of the narrative being used to express something important to the writer.

Comment

The evidence of this sample of written narratives indicates a progression from the simple chronicle of events, through simple stories based on a disruption of the probabilities, to more highly developed stories. The latter may contain not only more elaboration for the reader but also, in many cases, more than one level of storying — either the stories of events and of emotions, or the stories at the literal and symbolic levels.

It is particularly interesting to note that in all age groups of writers the third assignment, of writing for a very young audience, seemed meaningful. Amongst the youngest writers this task allowed many of the children their greatest success, whilst among the oldest writers it produced the more exciting developments in terms of symbolism. One might speculate that not only did this task offer the writer a genre model which stirred up ideas for content but that also offered an organisational blueprint based on their notions of 'what a story ought to be like'. This we shall discuss in the next chapter.

10 The organisation of narrative by 7–13-year-olds

Features of organisation

A well-formed text will contain a high degree of structure and organisation, as essential as the bones beneath the flesh, yet just as invisible. The skill of the proficient writer at concealing the bones may serve also to mask the difficulties faced by the child. Organisation is crucial in writing for whatever purpose and may be exceedingly difficult to achieve. Yet the nature of narrative and storying offer the learner-writer two sources of support not available in expository writing. One is that the sequence of narrative events lends its own degree of structure to the content. The other is the mental blueprint or story schema that the child is likely to have acquired already and researchers have analysed such story schemata in some detail.

The work of Rumelhart (1975) is often referred to in this connection. He maintains that, '[j]ust as simple sentences can be said to have an internal structure so too can stories be said to have an internal structure . . . the notion of well-formedness is nearly as reasonable for stories as it is for sentences' (p. 211). Thus he proposes what is modishly called a grammar, or set of rules, for accounting for the structure of simple stories in a hierarchical manner. Work by Mandler and Johnson (1977) and Stein and Glenn (1979) continues the discussion on story grammars or story schemata. Children would appear to acquire information about stories by hearing them, and to acquire information about causal relationships and sequences of action through experience of life, and thus they build up their own internal blueprint to aid them in processing and understanding further stories that they encounter.

The hierarchical tree of Stein and Glenn (1979) is an illustration of the type of structure proposed. They say that a story contains a setting and episode(s). The major setting is the introduction of the main character, while the minor setting contains other information regarding time, place and situation. The scene having been set, the episode is then allowed to

114

occur. The episode represents a complete, logically related sequence of behaviour, the initiating event provoking all that follows in terms of a plan of action and the eventual resolution of the story.

The relevant question in this research relates to children's ability to create a logically complete structure when asked to produce narrative, rather than process a received story. It is a matter alluded to briefly by Stein and Glenn (1979) in their conclusion. They indicate that children appear to experience great difficulty in this area, and frequently omit logically necessary categories of the idealised story blueprint. The description of developing episodic structure offered in this paper has been influenced by these arguments, as well as by descriptions of the structure or oral narratives given by Labov and Waletsky (1967), Labov (1977) and Kernan (1977).

These researchers tabulate their categories as containing the answers to questions the listener might pose:

1. Abstract: what was this about?
2. Orientation: who/when/where/what situation?
3. Complicating action: then what happened?
4. Evaluation: fending off 'so what?'.
5. Result of resolution: what finally happened?

A sixth category, a coda, may present a general comment or summing up, or serve to bring the listener from the end of the narrative right up to the present.

With such studies as background we drew up a category of 'organisation' in our research, sub-divided as beginners, settings, episodic structure, chronology and endings. It must be noted that one phrase in a text may serve more than one function in the structure. The model is set out in full below.

Beginnings. These are the devices, from the conventional ('Once upon a time . . .') to the individual, enabling the reader to enter into the time sequence at the start of the narrative.

Settings/orientation. On the one hand there are minimal settings, usually at the beginning; on the other increasingly relevant, detailed settings, integrated into the text where they become necessary to the narrative.

Episodic structure. At first there may be a largely temporal sequence of events which moves towards an increasingly logical sequence or sequences of behaviour.

Chronology. Devices for handling and varying the chronology basic to narrative grow more sophisticated.

Endings. Development in devices for concluding the narrative (from just stopping to shaping the conclusion) and making an exit from the time sequence.

Organisation in children's writing

Let us illustrate these features. The data used is that obtained in the investigation described in the previous chapter.

In our analysis we have in mind that one phrase may serve more than one function, and for instance, those phrases which provide an entry into the narrative are usually seen also to constitute a part of the setting or orientation for the reader. Again, elements noted here as having structural significance in the episode will be seen to be often the same elements noted in the previous chapter for their semantic role in the development of meaningful storying.

Beginnings and settings

Beginning devices show a high degree of consistency, whether they are of the stylised story-marker type, 'once upon a time . . .', or more individualised among older pupils. The majority lead the reader into the narrative by some direct reference to 'time', this being one of the features of the setting or orientation, along with details of character and place. Even amongst writings by the oldest children, introduction into the time sequence is favoured over putting character or place first (though character and place do provide the lead into some texts). The ability to realise the setting more fully with age is apparent, particularly in respect of the situation in which the characters find themselves. However, given the security of the traditional story form as perceived in the final writing assignment, some of the youngest writers achieve extremely full settings.

Beginnings and settings are often equated:

> It is Nicholas birthday today and she has got out of bed very early . . .
> Sarah (7)
> it was a dark misty morning and John and Kathy went down the steps into the alley way . . .
> Melanie (10)

Older writers may take great pains to present a setting before the initiation of events. Here is an example by Gregory (13):

> Set your minds back two hundred years, and you will find an old granary deep in the heart of one of old Englands most pleasant shires, Norfolk.

Episodic structure

Episodic structure is best illustrated by examples quoted at length. With young children a basic structure is a chain of events in time, where none of the events represent a full sequence of behaviour. It is the typical structure for conveying a chronicle and is illustrated in a text by Joanne (7):

Yesterday me and my family went out to the Horsford wood me and my brother climbed trees my brother was dressed up as a army-man then it was time to go home then we went to my nannys and had tea then . . .

In contrast an incomplete episode suggests more than the temporal chain. Some element in it is identifiable as prompting what follows. Joanne F. writes briefly in this form:

Yesterday I went round my nanne becaus nanny couldn't get her breath back mummy got a cream cake the doctor came to see my nanny she was better the next day and I helped my mum to do the cooking I made a orange cakes. the end.

The essence of the episode lies in nanny's illness initiating what follows, in terms of the visit, the doctor calling, and the recovery the next day. It is possible to begin to summarise the main points of an episode, even an incomplete one as in Joanne's composition, whereas in a temporal chain it is possible only to list the events in order.

There is evidence among the narratives of some seven-year-olds of development towards a more complete episodic structure, as well as instances of two episodes being temporally linked.

Episodic structure is perceptibly tighter and more fully formed amongst writers of ten years of age. Instances may be found of narratives that contain episodes linked by more than temporal ordering. The first episode allows the next to happen by setting up the situation. Again this is most readily illustrated by reference to a specific story, an imaginative narrative by Tina (10):

The Magic Puppet

Setting	Once upon a time, there was a little girl whose name was Victoria, she was only five. Her father was a ventriloquist and was trying to teach his daughter ventriloquism.
Event that initiates a response	One day Victorias father was teaching her when their dog brought the paper in, Victoria's father set down to read the news when he came across a box and in the box it said: A puppet for you ventriloquists. Phone: Skegness 401223, address: 6 Albert Road.
Response — an internal plan is implicit	Victorias father jumped up, 'Put your coat on we're of to the nearest phone box.

The plan is applied, though only partially revealed	Victoria put her coat on and her father rolled up the newspaper and they both raced down to the telephone box. When they got there they phoned up the lady in Skegness and asked how much the puppet was. Victoria was sent out of the phone box and her father spoke to the lady.
Resolution	Three days later the postman came and gave Victoria the parcel, when she opened it, it was nothing else but the puppet that her father had phoned up about.
Consequence	She played with it all day when she went to bed she sat it on a box.
This allows the next episode to occur: Initiating event	In the morning when she woke up she found that her puppet had moved from its box and was now sitting on the chair talking to one of her toys and laughing.
Response	She backed away and shouted 'Daddy help me, my puppet has come alive.'
Resolution	All of a sudden the puppet fell over and out from behind the chair came Victoria's father, he had been working with the puppet for a show he was doing.
Reaction	But for some reason Victoria never did want to be a ventriloquist again.

In structural terms, it is the initiating event that provokes what follows. Similarly, in storying terms it is the disturbance of probability which entails what follows. In the foregoing story, the two episodes are clearly linked by more than mere temporal order, and each episode may be traced from an initiating event to its completion.

Observable development in the structuring of episodes continues in the narrative writing of 13-year-olds. Episodes within a story become fully formed and coherently, logically linked. Whereas in Tina's story the internal plan and its application, regarding buying the puppet, are partly implicit (perhaps deliberately to increase anticipation and the eventual impact of the resolution), in 13-year-olds' texts internal planning, its application and results may be clearly specified. David makes his decisions and tactical plans explicit when tackling an 800-metre race, and the results are successful. Not all attempts to execute plans are immediately successful, as Kay (13) indicates. In her story, centred on a birthday present, the scene is ably set for the initiating event — the opening of the last and biggest parcel. An ugly doll or dummy with 'large glassy eyes' is revealed. The doll has come from New Zealand. A succession of misfortunes are then attributed to the doll's influence, until finally a plan to burn the doll is executed, with only partial success. The glassy eyes remain. This prompts a further plan (based on an internal reaction of greed, specified in the text) to have the 'eyes' valued by a jeweller. The revelation that the stones are Maori good luck stones that bring misfortune to non-Maoris, leads to the final resolution — to bury the stones, sell the farm and move away. Thus, the texts of the oldest writers demonstrate confident handling of complete behavioural sequences in closely related episodes.

Chronology
Organisation of the time sequence is seen to be strictly chronological in the majority of the narratives of seven-year-olds in the sample. Many writers seem to be controlled by the passage of time in strict order, with meal times, bed times, and so on, made explicit, to show time passing, up to and including the age of 13. However, ability to control the time sequence rather than be controlled by it, begins to be exhibited, at sentence level, in the writing of some ten-year-olds. Peter (10+) uses retrospection in recalling the career of a ventriloquist that leads to fame and fortune. Simon realises the simultaneity of events: Tommy, the boy in his story, plays with his puppet and '*Meanwhile* his mother got up and made a good Dinner'. Similarly Melanie records the utterances of a little creature when captured by a boy called Robin, She cannot record the creature's utterance and Robin's reaction simultaneously, so handles it thus:

> Now all this had taken Robin by surprise so he had just stood there with his mouth open, at last found his tongue.

In another of her texts Melanie shifts from immediate action to retrospection, back to immediate action, and then simultaneity, without difficulty, all within a few lines of text.

Retrospect, prospect and simultaneity occur at sentence level in examples of the oldest pupils' work. Stephen looks forward to the next day, but the prospect is imperfectly achieved since it is coloured by his knowledge of what the next day turned out to be like, as well as the expectation of what it would be like:

> When we got back we were absolutely exhausted. We wanted to go to bed early that night because the following day was even more exhausting.

There is a considerable cognitive load involved in manipulating the time span and pacing revelations for the reader when the narrator is in possession of full knowledge throughout.

Substantial manipulation of chronology occurs in a limited number of narratives. James (13+) includes a substantial section of retrospect, vital to the point of the narrative, in the middle of his text. However, the most radical manipulation is in a story by Graeme, in response to the picture of a distressed woman and her children. The narrative begins:

> When I told Sandra Blake she felt terrible. Her husband's death had shocket her . . . As the fact that her Simon was dead sunk in she remembered how it all began.

The narrator then tells retrospectively of the beginning of an imaginery war with Russia, and of submarine action in the Baltic. The narrator's role as friend and fellow crew-member of the ill-fated Simon become clear, and the narrative is led back to the point in time where Sandra received the news of his death, whereupon she

> asked me what to do, I told her this: Go out and find someone else and live your life.

And finally:

> I think she took my advice for in today's post brought me an invitation to her wedding to pilot Officer Joe Hastings.

The reader is brought up to date, and a chapter of Sandra's life is dealt with.

Endings

The organisation of endings of narratives rests to a large extent on the logicality or otherwise of what has gone before. In the simplest chronicles or stories embedded in chronicles, bedtime forms a convenient exit from the time sequence, while stories of younger writers may end abruptly at the point of resolution. Standard exists, such as 'happily ever after' and tag endings (the End) occur most frequently in the work of seven-year-olds (except where deliberately employed by older children to suit the task set). Amongst the middle age group, brief summary or evaluation begins to occur:

> I vowed that I would never go fishing with emma again   (Sonia, 10)

> It was a great game.   (Darren, 10)

> That is how the woodland fold had a newcomer.   (Paul, 10)

The coda to bring the reader up to date, or allow the narrator to address the reader directly, is more typical of the older writers, as in this text by Neil (12.11):

We are now thinking of doing a sponsored cycle ride round Norfolk for the Big C appeal.

or in Rachel's ending:

I wouldn't believe a story like that, would you?

(Rachel 12.9)

Kay offers her reader a final warning:

If you ever plan to buy a small-holding farm in Suffolk just ask the estate agent why the previous occupants sold it.

(Kay 13+)

The texture of narrative

Two of the basic facts about human beings are that they exist; and that they act; two more facts are that these happen in time and space. Thus in reading stories we can examine how these things are conveyed. So we can look at:

1. The events, what actually happens (core narrative).
2. The descriptions, what things are like.
3. The time and order in which the events are presented.
4. The space, environment, place, in which the events happen.

Let us take a piece of composition by Christopher, aged 6:

Our dog got lost my dad fund him

and let us analyse this composition under the four headings 'events' (core narrative), 'description' (explanation), 'time' and 'space':

Our dog got lost
my dad fund him

There is only event. This is partly because, with young children, the effort of producing that, without additional description, is quite sufficient.

Let us take a piece of composition by Moira, aged seven:

Events	Description	Time	Place
I got up and got dressed and went down and had my breakfast			
	it was frosties		
then we went shopping with daddy car then we came home and had dinner			(home)

In the afternoon

I played with
my friend

We played skip-
ping and dolls

Her mother said
come for tea so
she went so I
had my tea and
watched Dr who
then I went to
bed.

This composition is predominantly chronological — a listing of events, just because they occurred, not because of the particular interest of any one of them, but there are two pieces of explicit description, which give some picture to the reader. There is one indication of the time, though of course the information is implicit elsewhere. There are two mentions of place ('daddy car' and 'home'). The time sequence is chronological. This type of composition, where the events through the day are listed, is known for obvious reasons as a 'bed-to-bed' composition.

Let us look at a piece, already touched on (p. 17) by Pauline, aged nine:

Events	Description	Time	Place
	I had just	(had)	
	moved into a		
	new house.		
	I had no friends		
	My sister was		
	only about four		
	years old I		
	looked for some		
	friends but I		
	couldn't find any		
Then I heard a			
noise			
	someone was	(was)	
	bouncing		on a matrue
then I looked			
over the wall			
and there			
I found some-			
body I said			
Who are you?			
what is your			
name? She said			
the same to me			

it was my old
friend I knew
in play school
(she is in this
school now) she
is called nicola
Thorn   (suspense
                              resolved)

We played
skipping   until it was
                              time for me to
                              go in

I had my tea
and I watched
television and
I went to bed ...

In this story there is still some repetition of chronological events for the sake of completeness, notably the last sentence. On the other hand the proportion of event to description has changed. Pauline is as much concerned with interesting readers by setting the scene, by explaining, by giving a context in time and space.

A very interesting development is that Pauline is not completely bound by the chronological sequence. The actual events of the story start with the noise. But before that she has taken us back into the past (what 'had' happened before) in order to sketch in the background. Again she does not give us information in the order in which she was aware of it in the incident. Clearly she remembered Nicola's name when she saw her, but she withholds this information from us, referring only to seeing 'somebody', gradually giving us more information, and then eventually the name — 'she is called nicola Thorn'. She was much more able to select information of interest than Moira, the seven-year-old, was.

The device of raising the reader's curiosity by giving a little information is one of the means writers use to build up interest or suspense. It implies the ability to manipulate not just to follow chronology, and is of course a stylistic feature.

Catherine, aged ten, pushes the balance still further over towards the descriptive elements. The events, core narrative, begins conventionally — getting up and dressed, going downstairs to breakfast; but after that information is much more sparse: 'We got into the car . . . we went into a room. . . . We went along to a door. . . . A small dog walket out dad paid the man . . . we named the dog'. The narration is strictly chronological and some unnecessary details are included.

One morning I woke up to find mum shouting "Helen time to get up,"
"Okay". I got dressed and went downstairs. I found mum cooking

breakfast. I sat down, and poured out the cornflakes. "Mum where's the milk." The milk man hasent been yet. "Drats". I poured the cornflakes back into the packet. Buy the time I had done that because they cep't on farling out. Mum had placet my breakfast on the table. It was fried egg on toast the toast was a little burnt. It was February and today we were going to Exeter, we were going to get my dog that day. Dad came in with Honey woof went Honey. Then it was time to go. We got into the car and then were on are way there. When we got there we went into a room. There was a old lady on the floor scrubbing with a foaming brush. The floor was covered with newspaper the old lady told us to stand on the newspaper so we did. Then a man came in he looket at us. "Hellow,". He said he took us along lots of cells with dogs jumping up at the doors. The rooms were about a metre wide. We went along to a door and the man opened it. A small dog walket out dad paid the man then we went home we named the dog Petra she was beautiful.

Very little is necessary in the way of explanation to the reader as a series of simple events is being described which present no problems of understanding. But the great strength of this piece is its description. The family atmosphere is created partly by the breakfast dialogue; partly by the choice of significant detail — Helen 'poured the cornflakes back into the packet' — with nice touches of humour. And later in the piece there are sentences included purely for their pictorial detail: 'There was an old lady on the floor scrubbing with a foaming brush' and 'The floor was covered with a newspaper'. The description is marked by a sense of objectivity, as though Catherine is seeing herself and the incidents through the eyes of a third party.

Catherine's piece demonstrates considerable confidence in description, but its presence in the early part tends to unbalance the piece, and the later events are on the whole listed rather than described. In contrast, by the age of 18 a writer like John is in control of core narrative in relation to description, he is able to suggest place as appropriate; above all his use of the time sequence is not mechanically chronological:

Being lost is an experience which one does not like to encounter frequently. Being lost when nobody finds you is worse. It was during our holidays in South Devon, when we were out for the day, when it started. I had decided to walk from the car, intending to be picked up later. Naturally, I took the turning from which we had come, the car however didn't. I began to feel a little uneasy as the time passed, and the tall hedges produced wild thoughts in my mind. Drizzle floated to the ground.

I'm not sure how far I walked that evening, it seemed miles I had cut across fields and had become wet. On reaching a house, I knocked on the door, for by this time I was very worried. When it was answered I asked the way to the town at which we were staying. I was offered a lift and accepted it gratefully. The next part I cannot remember.

I do remember regaining consciousness and peering through a smashed

windscreen at a crowd gathered outside. I kept perfectly still, least any bone should be broken. I vaguely remember the journey in an ambulance and the kindness of the ambulance men. My mother and father were at the hospital. Mother looked relieved yet shocked at the same time. (I can't have looked very pretty).
My shoulder was very painful, but the cuts on my face were numb. After being x-rayed I had my cuts stitched (very painful). I was in hospital for the rest of our holiday.

The core narrative would seem to be as follows: 'I took the turning . . . the car however didn't. I walked that evening . . . On reaching a house, I knocked on the door . . . I asked the way . . . I was offered a lift and accepted it . . . I kept perfectly still . . . the journey in an ambulance . . . the hospital . . . after being x-rayed I had my cuts stitched . . . I was in hospital'. The most notable variation in the time sequence is the break between paragraphs two and three, so that description of the accident is omitted. It required considerable self-control on the part of a writer to exclude what would have been the natural climax in the interests of a more exact presentation of his own experience. A second variation is provided by the retrospective statements such as: 'I had decided to walk down from the car.' and 'I had cut across the fields and become very wet.' A second narrative is implied as much as stated in the actions of his parents who presumably were in the car which missed him, and are in the background until they appear at the hospital.

The more mature the writer the more likely the core narrative is to be accompanied by explanations as well as description. This writer is very aware of his readers. A variety of different explanatory devices is used to evaluate the experience for them. The piece opens with a generalisation about being lost which sets a context for what follows: 'Being lost when nobody finds you is worse.' There then comes an explanation of the location: 'It was during our holidays in South Devon.' followed by an account of the motive for the writer's action — he had hoped to be picked up by the car. He was not, and the absence of explanation here is deliberate, adding to the air of suspense. After this there is little explicit explanation, except 'for by this time I was very worried' and 'least any bone should be broken'. Nevertheless a rational world is implied — his mother's shock is obviously partly related to his experience.

A characteristic of this place is the number of descriptive features. The opening sentence is echoed with modification in the second sentence for stylistic effect. Again, the writer conveys to us his psychological state in terms of details from the natural environment: 'the tall hedges produced wild thoughts in the mind. Drizzle floated to the ground.' He allows the pictorial detail of the 'smashed windscreen' through which he peers to symbolise the accident and its confusing effects. His choice of vocabulary is exact and compelling — 'uneasy', 'wild thoughts', 'drizzle floated', 'very worried', 'gratefully', 'peering', 'crowd gathered', 'vaguely remembered', 'relieved yet shocked', 'very painful', 'numb'.

Patterns of chronology

The following patterns cover the arrangement of chronology in this age range:

1. Where an aggregate of sentences including some temporal junctures has inconsistencies in time and tense.
2. Simple linear pattern, narrative begins at the beginning, relating events in strict order with consistent use of tense.
3. Straight sequential pattern may be interrupted at sentence level to include brief retrospection or anticipation, then returns to sequential relation. Tenses usually handled appropriately.
4. Ability to portray simultaneity of events.
5. Writer begins main narrative by plunging *in medias res* and after orientating reader to time, place, character and some events, fills in the gaps by extensive retrospection. Some use of prospect, though less sustained than retrospection.
6. Narrative commences with the final scenario and then a complete flashback to the beginning and relation of events in order of time brings reader up to date.
7. Overall competence in handling chronology is such that writer can operate choice, and is not bound by the strait-jacket of time, but can make it a tool of organising the tale as he deems appropriate.

Most of these patterns have been been illustrated in this chapter. The simple linear pattern is represented by Moira's bed-to-bed story (p. 121–2). The incidental retrospection interrupting a linear pattern is seen in Pauline's piece (p. 122–3). James flashes back from a final scene (p. 120). Overall competence in handling time by means of choice comes with a more mature writer like John (pp. 124–6).

Comment

At the beginning of this chapter we spoke of the two sources of support available to the writer of narrative which is absent in other modes, such as the varied types of discursive writing. These are the temporal arrangement of events in life; and the story schemes likely to be available in the culture. These two facts underlie our discussion of composition in this chapter, and are the reason we have paid such attention to chronology as a basic organising principle. Narrative is bound to be the easiest and earliest form of writing, as it is the most enjoyable. Parents read a bedtime story to children, and both enjoy it. It is far less common for them to read a bedtime argument.

11 The writing curriculum

Introduction

The original study, which became known as the Crediton Project (Wilkinson *et al.*, 1980) suggested a way of looking at written composition which would bring out features of its development in the work of writers between seven and 14. Little was known about such development, and traditional marking schemes were far too narrow to say much of significance about it, so the Crediton models of cognition, affect, morals and style were devised. Both research and development work since that time have confirmed their value. Let us consider examples of each.

A notable study by Carlin (1986) compared results on count measures as in Harpin's system (1976) with those on Crediton criteria. Over a six-year period he had monitored children from age seven, and found that their development on sentence and clause length, and amount and variety of embedding, increased steadily. He concluded that such measures provide useful *general* information, irrespective of sex. However, writers with very similar count scores may differ considerably on Crediton measures. Carlin instances two boys as representative, one of whom, with greater count scores, was nevertheless more limited in affective development, organisation, vocabulary and reader awareness. He concludes (Carlin, 1986, p. 22):

> It seems obvious that count measures, useful as they are as indicators of *group trends*, provide an inadequate description of individual writer/writing development. An abbreviated version of the Wilkinson models for the analysis of writing would seem to offer more scope for assessing individual writer/writing development.

The comment on the usefulness of an abbreviated model is one we shall take up later in the chapter.

As far as curriculum development is concerned there have been extensive courses and workshops in Australia, Canada, and the United Kingdom. Hastings County, Ontario, with the notable work of Marshall (1985), should be particularly mentioned as having built the Crediton concepts into their language curriculum. All this activity has greatly clarified the implications of the Crediton Project, particularly for the classroom. We shall discuss the two major implications: for the nature of the writing curriculum, and for its assessment.

The classification of writing tasks

There are various ways of classifying composition. A basic one is by subject. A teacher asking the very understandable question, what on earth shall I give them to write about today? is probably classifying in this way. The problem is a permanent one. Over 70 years ago Fowler (1932, p. 22) wrote amusingly about 'the difficulty of finding subjects within the capacity of the pupil' and how the teacher would come up with 'How I spent my summer holidays' in September, and 'How I spent my Christmas holidays' in January. Traditionally associated with this classification by subject is one by form or genre — a poem, a report, a letter, a short story, and so on. These and other classifications are usefully discussed in Harpin (1976, p. 38 ff).

More recent classifications have tended to arise under the influence of socio-linguistics which we spoke about above — those which describe by function or purpose, often in relation to a specified reader (or audience). Thus the APU, for its work on national assessment, employs the functions of: reporting/recording; explaining/instructing; planning; describing; requesting; arguing/persuading; narrating; expression of feelings/personal reflection (APU, 1984, pp. 91–2). All classifications have their limitations. As Davis *et al.* (1978, p. 17) point out: 'Function on its own . . . is not a satisfactory criterion for judging style or mode, as an apparently identical function may have linguistically different realisations.' The Davis team offer a well-argued taxonomy developed from the rhetorical categories — narrative, descriptive, argumentative, expository, etc.

There are, however, classifications which are not in terms of topics, are not literary, and are not sociolinguistic, concerned with the writer's development. Thus Sanders (1966) breaks down mental activities into various levels; memory, translation, interpretation, application, analysis, synthesis, evaluation. In *Focus on Writing* (Ontario Ministry of Education, 1982, p. 6) writing activities which may be associated with each are given. We may quote two examples:

Translation	envisages information	describes an object;
	envisages in a form	records an experiment;
	represented in a form	writes labels; records
	other than the original	measurements; draws
		a picture of an event;
		graphs information;
		writes captions; writes
		out an interview; makes
		a model of an Indian
		village

Synthesis	uses original thought to solve a problem	writes poetry (haiku); designs and carries out an experiment; writes a story of a fictional event; paints in response to music; rewrites an ending to a story; writes in response to music; writes what came before a story started

Clearly the activities are not confined to the English lesson; but may occur anywhere in the curriculum where 'composing' is found.

Behind all teaching there is a classification of some kind. Creative writing, for instance, has been popular since the 1960s in the earlier years of schooling; but it also implies at least one other category of writing which is in some sense not creative, 'uncreative writing', dismissively called 'recording' (see p. 26 above). This is a 'genre' classification. Teachers are often unaware that they are making classifications. They tend, very naturally, to think in terms of what will work, what will interest and excite the pupils. If they follow through themes, or projects, they are more often concerned with the end-products of these, the motivations and satisfactions of the children, than in more closely defined objectives. A teacher, like a novelist, often starts with an intuition about a situation which will produce valuable writing.

This is of course very proper, indeed essential. However, to see its limitations we need to start at the other end, and ask what it leaves out. If for instance we asked ourselves the question about the written language of a group of pupils, what functions are not covered, then we may find there are several, as judged by the APU list referred to above. A similar question about 'mental activities' may throw up even more omissions.

Any classification of writing tasks implies a particular view of the learner. A classification by genre has in the past implied a view of the learner as recipient of traditional wisdom, particularly as represented by literature. A classification into creative writing and 'uncreative writing' (by default) implies a learner who is a 'poetic spirit' rather than a practical being. A classification by function sees the learner operating in a social world with perhaps less time for literature or personal contemplation. A psychological classification is different again. The one we quoted emphasises the 'mental activities' being developed in the writing (Sanders, 1966) — the learner is envisaged as a thinking being developing through various means, including writing.

The classification in terms of 'mental activities' is one in the spirit of our research, but the implications of the Crediton study are for a much more comprehensive classification or 'taxonomy' of written discourse.

The Crediton Taxonomy of written discourse

In Wilkinson *et al.* (1980, p. 223) we wrote:

> In English teaching there are various basic assumptions: one or more of
> these influence the teaching whether the particular teacher can formulate
> it explicitly or not. We have preferred that which regards the child as a
> 'communicative being', emphasising both 'communicating' and 'being'.

The stylistic model was concerned with the communicating, the cognitive,
affective and moral with the 'being', with psychological processes. Apart
from the work of Taylor (1986) there has been no research on style since
the original study (Wilkinson and Hanna, 1980). We shall thus base what
follows on the other three categories of the Crediton model.

Table 3 shows what a classification of writing tasks based on the
Crediton psychological processes would look like.

Table 3: Crediton taxonomy of written discourse

Function	Activity*	Example†
Cognitive		
Reporting	Selectivity	Annual report
Planning	Hypothesis and prediction	Five-year plan
Arguing	Weighing evidence	Public enquiry — judgement
Explaining	Entering mind of reader	Textbook
Persuading	Sensing others' attitudes	Charity letter
Classifying	Organising in Categories	Flora
Affective		
Reflecting	Discovering self-awareness	Diary
Empathising	Entering the uniqueness of others	Novel
Setting	Interacting with non-human phenomena	Fable
Coping	Defining stance towards the human condition	Poem
Moral		
Evaluating	Appraising experience in terms of a moral universe	Parable

* No single function involves one mental activity only, but we list only one for
convenience
† A single instance of where one *might* find such activity is given as an
example.

It might seem at first sight as if this were just another function model, but that is far from being the case. It contains a list of functions, certainly, but there are considerably extended from (say) that of the APU, in the fields of affect and morals. The major difference however, lies in the way these functions are considered as psychological activities, and the scheme (the Crediton models) by which they are evaluated, and evaluated in detail. What is not perceived by an evaluating instrument is, effectively, not present.

In listing the functions and associated activities in this way we are not suggesting that they should necessarily be taught as though they were separate items, though drawing attention to the particular qualities that are expected in a certain composition is a way of developing these ('Concentrate on getting the argument clear', 'Try to bring out what you felt . . .'). Nor are we suggesting for one moment that writing can be taught unrelated to discussion and other experiences, particularly reading. Often a 'theme', 'topic', or 'project' is the best means of developing the various activities.

Thus a group of experienced teachers discussing the implementation of Crediton gave as an example the theme of law and order with older secondary school pupils in mind:

	Law and order
Argument, planning, classifying, moral	Evaluation of the severity of ten crimes, using small groups to discuss, but subsequently leading to individual decisions.
Argument, moral, affective (others and human condition)	Should the punishment fit the crime?
Argument, planning moral	Arguments for and against corporal/capital punishment perhaps in preparation for discussion or debate. A 'crime' staged without warning in front of the class. Pupils report on what they witnessed individually, and the reports then compared for 'accuracy'.
All affective categories. Moral argument, report planning, explanation	Letter from a delinquent to a magistrates' court; or to a close friend.
Moral, affect (self, others) report	Write about the unfairest treatment you have been given or have given to others.

Such tasks would be carried out in a context of appropriate background reading and stimulus material. Other examples of how practising teachers perceive items in the taxonomy being manifested in the classroom are given in the Appendix.

Assessment of written composition

The original Crediton team wrote of their assessment models (Wilkinson *et al.*,). 1980, p. 223):

> the models are not meant for use as a day-to-day marking scheme. The teachers who co-operated with us in the project were firmly against any summary or simplification which might seem to imply this. They felt that one of the strengths of the models lay in their detail which paid due regard to the varieties of activity going on in the process of writing.

This remains true. It is clear that to fully recognise the features of a composition one needs to do a detailed analysis of it. Since the models contain a total of 100 items this might seem a formidable task, though teachers in workshops over the past five years have found no difficulty in acquiring a working knowledge of the application of the models. Once such a process has been undergone then the criteria are internalised and become part of one's mental equipment for impression marking. This certainly is the most desirable state of affairs.

Nevertheless it has to be said that, in the last resort, it is the attitude towards writing that Crediton implies, rather than its detailed categorisation, that is important and we noted above Carlin's advocacy of an 'abbreviated version' (Carlin, 1986, p. 184). Wilcock (1985) asked teachers to respond to written work on their own criteria; he then explained the *general* principles of the Crediton approach to them, and reported that their subsequent responses revealed a revaluation of the compositions in more positive and exact terms, perceiving a wider range of features.

These are the kinds of change one would hope for. Much traditional marking practice prompts markers to be negative, seeking mistakes, and if they look for formal features such as spelling and punctuation this is very easy to do. It also prompts them to be punitive. This matter is little spoken of but somewhere deep in some markers there is rejection of the writer's perceived rivalry; otherwise why all the blood on the page disguised as red pencil marks?

And again traditional practice prompts markers to be grudging; it is unusual for the writer of a composition ever to get any where near full marks, and in many examinations 70% is 'first class'. It is as though, one day, someone will write the composition to end all compositions, the trumpets will sound, and the ultimate mark, specially preserved for the occasion, will be awarded. This feature of marking tends to occur when the purpose is to arrange the writers in order of merit, as in a test.

Crediton is not a testing instrument but a teaching instrument, that is, it aims to make assessments of the individual development of children's writing in order to help them to develop further. Its use implies a positive attitude.

With these considerations in mind let us then attempt to present the Crediton approach non-technically but in a way which will not do a disservice to the distinctive features it contains.

An assessment scheme for written composition

The scheme cannot be used to give marks, only to make a profile of development in four local areas. No composition should be squeezed into any one category against its will; for instance, there may be aspects of all four cognitive activities in a single composition.

In cognition and morals the items in the left-hand column are in developmental sequence; in affect and style they are not, and may be present simultaneously.

Cognition

Describing	Writing in which information is offered or a report given without any attempt at interpretation or explanation. This has been called 'knowledge telling' (Biggs, forthcoming) or 'describer thinking' (Peel, 1971). Poor 'describing' would be marked by, for example, too little information, too much information (showing an inability to select), incorrect information (lack of knowledge), vague information (lack of accuracy).
Interpreting	Writing in which information is offered with explanations; in which deductions are drawn. Poor 'interpreting' would be marked by inadequate premises, or illogical inferences.
Generalising	Writing which shows the ability to draw information together. Simple plurals do this (e.g. 'children like games') but of course these are only at very elementary level. More advanced forms are the ability to summarise complex information, to draw conclusions based on it, to classify it. The level of the generalising is related to the complexity and degree of abstraction of the information dealt with.

Speculating   The writing in which hypotheses are created and deductions drawn from them. Even very young children can make hypotheses ('if I'm good I can stay up'.) At the highest level we are concerned with 'hypothetico-deductive' thinking in which sustained theorising is possible about a complex of variables. Substantial arguments leading to conclusions.

Affect

Self   Writers first express their thoughts and feelings unselfconsciously. They gradually become more aware of their own motives, the image they present, their effect on others.

Others   Others first appear in writing as cut-out figures; they begin to assume three dimensions, become realised ('made real') as people. Empathy with them as unique individuals develops. In literature this appears as an ability to 'draw character'.

Environment   Human beings develop a relation with the non-human phenomena of the world, their response to 'things being various' which may be from 'sketching in the background on the one hand to a symbolic use of environment on the other.

Human Condition   The constant pressure of 'coming to terms with reality' can often be most thoughtfully carried out and understood in writing, in terms, for instance, of 'coping' and 'defending'.

Morals

People see an action as 'valid' or 'justified' in terms of something else, which 'validates' it. The validation of an action, in developmental order, is in terms of:

Self-gratification 'I wanted it, so I took it'.

Rewards   'The well behaved go home early; the others stay in!'

Social approval   'If you don't behave Mummy will be upset!'

Conventional	'It's against the Law to steal'. 'It's not fair!'
Motivation	'I didn't intend to knock him down — I was pushed!'
Right and wrong	'Murder is wrong'. Notice how this differs from the other validations. The murderer cannot argue in justification that he wanted to, that he would be rewarded, that his social group approved, that this law gave sanction, even that the murder was a result rather than the intention of his action. All these arguments might admittedly be used by a country using terrorism as an agent of international policy. They are however almost universally rejected.

Style

Organisation	The most elementary continuous written arrangement of words in practice is chronology, which becomes narrative. Narrative need not remain chronological and more mature writers manipulate the temporal sequence, omitting, and reordering. Other forms of organisation emerge in relation to the needs of the writing. It seems, for example, that in its way a pro/con pattern is as basic for argument as chronology is for narrative.
Cohesion	Whereas organisation is the timber or steel framing, cohesion is the mortar that bonds the bricks. Cohesive devices range from simple conjunctions and pronouns to sophisticated literary devices — parallelism, contrast, assonance, alliteration, etc.
Syntax	Younger children use simple sentences. They may seem to write very long sentences but these are at bottom simple sentences without punctuation. Subordinate clauses are a sign of development. Those beginning with 'when' and 'if' come much earlier than those beginning with 'unless' and 'although'. Mature writers may use parts of sentences on their own as deliberate devices.

Lexis

Young writers have comparatively few words, some of the most common in the language, so they make them work hard. These are verbs like 'be', 'have', 'get', 'go', and their forms; nouns like 'man', 'lady', 'boy', 'girl', 'friend'; adjectives and adverbs are even fewer — 'happy', 'sad', 'few', 'very'. Then they acquire other words to give more particular meanings: Not just 'go' but 'run', 'walk', 'hurry', 'stagger'. Not just 'walk' but 'walk slowly'; not just 'stagger', but 'stagger drunkenly'.

Young writers use scarcely any metaphors except those in the language stock, such as 'quick as a flash'. More metaphorical language comes with adolescence when the act of writing gives an opportunity to reflect on more exact shades of language.

Reader

Writing has to be 'context free' in that the intended recipients are not immediately present as with speech. It has therefore to carry all the information necessary to understand it. Young children cannot do this; older children do it easily for the teacher. One educational problem comes in providing other readerships which are real. But another (which is what this book is concerned with) is to provide young writers with an opportunity to write for a reader who is the self.

Appropriateness

Writing is not written-down speech which is what young children make it. An early discovery must be that writing is different from speech. But then come a series of discoveries that writing is different from writing also — that there are a variety of forms of 'genres' each considered appropriate, because more efficient than others, for different purposes.

Except for style, for obvious reasons, the schemes will not apply equally to all modes of writing. One would expect affect in autobiography but not in the account of a laboratory experiment, for example. The cognitive scheme is apparently less applicable to creative than to discursive writing. Because writers express their ideas in concrete terms, as characters for instance, and leave a lot of the interpretation to the reader, we might be tempted to rate such work on the describing/reporting level, without even much interpretation, and not to find speculation or deduction in it. And this would seem to imply that such writing is not much of a cognitive activity. This would be wrong, however, Writers tend to express themselves in concrete terms, as in characters, not abstractions. It is part of the technique to present characters in interaction, without even much overt interpretation, so that a good deal is left to the reader. But a good deal of selection and interpretation has gone on behind the scenes before this stage is ever reached. Again, for writers the hypothetico-deductive operation is partly represented by propositions such as: given characters with certain features, how are they likely to behave over a period in relation to the 'complex of variables' called life? It is very doubtful whether such an analysis in these terms has ever been carried out. Not surprisingly it is far beyond the scope of the Crediton models, which must essentially be concerned with comparatively short stretches of text.

Since we have in this book demonstrated the application of a non-technical form of the assessment models on several occasions (particularly in Chapters 2, 3, 6, 7 and 8) we shall not do so again here. The use for them which we are suggesting is not to produce a mark for a grading scale, but to produce a range of evidence for an individual development profile. Thus 'Jim' is not 13/20 but 'conscious of the need to explain', 'becoming more self-aware'; 'Isabel' is not Grade C, but 'uses an effective metaphor', faces up to things'. CAMS (cognitive, affect, morals, style) provides a convenient mnemonic for the concerns of this approach.

Comment

We have argued in this chapter that the ideas developed in this book have implications both for the range of writing taught in the classroom, and for the ways in which it should be evaluated. The range of writing should provide more scope for the development of thinking, and feeling, and for moral growth than is sometimes the case. The mode of evaluation is necessarily related to these things. What we teach, is inseparable from our method of assessing it.

12 The last chapter

This is the end of the book. It is not only a book about writing. It is also a book about the human soul and how we should cherish it, in others and in ourselves.

Appendix

CREDITON IN THE CLASSROOM

Introduction

These suggestions for work along Crediton lines arise from seminar work by experienced teachers on the MA course in Language in Education at the University of East Anglia, 1984–5. Members of the course were: J. Bidwell; G. Coneys; W. Foot; B. Kulsdom; A. Littlefair; D. Metson; C. Onwere; H. Pearson; F. Rimmell; E. Watkins; J. Robinshaw; E. Wilcock; and M. Vigar. The simulation sections are the work of E. Wilcock.

The suggestions include both oral and written work because these obviously interact, and are meant to be considered only in a context of supporting material — factual/imaginative — in a range of media.

Activities involving cognitive, affective and moral aspects

Cognition

Argument

Seven-year-olds.
Group discussion – points written on 'pros and cons' sheet. Pair/individual work. *Look at each side of an argument separately.* Topics: 'Should we be allowed to bring sweets to school?' 'Is it right for children to be allowed to watch whatever they choose on television?'' 'Should children decide on their own bedtime?'

Ten-year-olds.
Vary time of discussion — sometimes before, sometimes after written work. *Still needs to be based on reality.* Topics: Pros and cons of building a bypass. Discussion of need for school rules. Mock elections involving written 'manfestos'. Working in groups and 're-porting back' generates ideas.

11-year-olds.
(*NB.* Much overlap here) Discussion of local (i.e. school and community) issues.

13-year-olds.
Should be able to argue at a more abstract level on occasion. Topics: For and against nuclear weapons. Merits of education for work or leisure. The values of homework. Should withdrawal of labour be forbidden by law? Should grandparents live within family unit?

Report

Seven-year-olds.
Needs to be an experience in the recent past, or imagination comes into play in excess. Topics: The journey to school. Weekend visitors. Shopping.

Ten-year-olds.
More able generally to separate fact from fantasy. Topics: The football match/netball match. The school party/disco. Project — school newspaper.

11-year-olds.
Work which will appeal to a wider audience: class/notice-board/open evening. Topics: A school visit/holiday. A report on a play or theatre visit. Book reviews.

Explanation

Seven-year-olds.
Try to make reasons for explanations purposeful, e.g. instructions that others need to follow. Illustrate. Topics: Class recipe book. Instructions for making 'Lego' models. Colour mixing instructions using primary colours.

Ten-year-olds.
Topics: Class book of games (invented or otherwise). PE instructions — e.g. how to do a forward roll. Science — e.g. why plants grow better in conditions of light and warmth.

11-year-olds.
Topics: How to load a program into a computer. Explaining a hobby or interest. Explaining mechanical processes, e.g. how a clock works, how a bicycle moves.

Planning and classification

Seven-year-olds.
Topics: Listing things needed for an activity — e.g. building a boat. Draw and describe setting up of an art table/wendy house/shop. Graphs, e.g. showing modes of transport to school. Shopping lists, equipment needed, e.g. for cookery.

Ten-year-olds.
Classify items on a nature table. Local history/geography — street or town study — past, present and future. Science — planning an experiment. Understanding how a library system works. 'How I would prepare my house for Christmas'.

11-year-olds.
Planning a day out for a friend from another town or country. Describe and illustrate a house of the future. How would you prepare an end of term party? Organising a camping holiday/school trip. 'How I would decorate my room'.

Persuasion

Seven-year-olds.
Topics: Letter writing — e.g. 'Please come to tea'. Persuade granny to buy a particular present. Asking an adult to help you learn to swim. A letter to 'Jim'll Fix It'.

Nine-year-olds.
A letter to a radio DJ with a request.

Ten-year-olds.
Topics: Letters, e.g. to county council: 'Please don't close our school'. To farmer: 'May I take a short cut across your field?' Project on advertising. A letter to a shop complaining about e.g. a broken toy. Classroom drama may be effective starting point.

11-year-olds.
Topics: In pairs write a dialogue between housewife and door-to-door salesman. (Tape record). A letter persuading a friend not to smoke/take drugs, etc. Letter requesting facilities in youth clubs, etc/requesting permission for a class visit. Letters of application.

Affect

Self:

Seven-year-olds.
'Helping at home'. 'When I grow up'. 'My favourite day of the week'. Diary.

Ten-year-olds.
'Most of all I enjoy . . . 'Watching the TV news: how it affects me'. 'Why I like/dislike school'. Diary.

11-year-olds.
'Am I looking forward to leaving school?' 'In my spare time . . .' Diary.

Others

Seven-year-olds.
My mummy/daddy/grandma/sister, etc. Why I like my friend.

Ten-year-olds.
Living as a handicapped person. My next-door neighbours. Being a policeman. Old age.

11-year-olds.
Relationships at home. Life in an institution/prison/children's home. Famine. 'The ideal friend'.

Environment

Seven-year-olds.
Poetry very useful here. Topics: My house. A tree — poem. Bonfire night.

Nine-year-olds.
'The Time Machine'.

Ten-year-olds.
Topics: Description of a visit to the church. 'Alone in the dark'. World War poetry (project) — 'A letter home from the trenches'. 'The Year 2000'. 'Shipwreck'.

Human condition

Seven-year-olds.
Literary based topics are suggested for all age groups. Become involved with charity work, e.g. Save the Children Fund.

Ten-year-olds.
Rules and regulations. Tramps and vagrants — the problem/possible solutions. Other 'outsiders' in society.

13-year-olds.
Old people in society. Projects: Crime/war/violence. Poverty and affluence in the world.

Moral Judgement

Seven-year-olds.
Topics: Issue of trespassing. Bible stories. Aesop's fables.

Ten-year-olds.
Topics: Discussion and written comment about reported court cases. Reconstruct a courtroom situation. Write 'modern' versions of Bible stories in play form, e.g. 'The Good Samaritan'. Class debates on topical issues.

13-year-olds.
The freedom to choose own clothes/TV/bedtimes/whether to smoke or not. Rights and wrongs of school punishment system. 'Speakers corner' — devise a speech about something you feel strongly about — class debates.

A language simulation

By using a stimulus such as a language simulation pupils are offered a context for their writing tasks.

In the 'Lowstead Airport' simulation pupils are asked to imagine that they are either 'The Chairperson of the Lowstead Residents' Committee' or 'A member of the Lowstead Resident Committee'.

The stimuli are as follows:

1. A Letter from Wingair Associates. This outlines their plans for developing a disused wartime airfield into a small airport and heliport.
2. A Letter from a local resident. This outlines the situation this resident will find herself in should the airport be developed. She also puts forward the case for the environmentalist.
3. A Map. This shows the village and the surrounding areas. It also shows the exact details of the proposed airport.
4. A Letter from the local publican. This is a letter agreeing to his pub being used for a meeting about the proposed airport.

Pupils may be asked to look at this simulation individually or in groups, depending on particular aims and objectives of the use of this simulation.

Below is catalogued the possible written work which could result from the use of this simulation in terms of Crediton.

Cognitive Mode

Argument	What are the 'pros' and 'cons' of the proposed airfield? (Advocate either view).
Report	Write a speech or report to be delivered at the AGM which informs people about the developments regarding the airfield. (This also is a good exercise in register.)
Explanation	Write a circular letter to those people who do not live in Lowstead who may be interested in the development of the airport, i.e. surrounding villagers. Give full details of the forthcoming meeting and a clear explanation of how to get to the Butcher's Arms.

Persuasion	Write a letter to the farmer asking him to delay any sale of land to Wingair Associates until the whole issue of the airport has been publicly discussed and researched.
Summary	Design a handbill advertising the forthcoming AGM of the Residents' Committee.
Planning	Make notes for a conversation (telephone) with Cecilia Hawksworth.
Classification	Write the agenda for the forthcoming AGM.

Affective Mode

Self	Imagine that you were in the position of Cecilia Hawksworth. How would you react to your house being destroyed and finding yourself being rehoused by the construction of an airport.
Others	Write a sympathetic letter to Cecilia Hawksworth saying that you will look into her plight and voice her sentiments at the forthcoming AGM.
Environment	See the first cognitive mode task.
Human condition	Mankind has come a long way from the cave age but, despite man's high technology, he is still not able to live in peace and happiness. Why do you think this is?

Moral Mode

What right does Cecilia Hawksworth have to stand in the way of progress (or the raft spider for that matter)? Give your thoughts on this subject.

Conclusions

Obviously one would not use the language simulation to go through the gamut of these proposed written tasks, but a selective use would prove valuable. The letters were first used as part of an examination. One interesting aspect of applying Crediton is that it draws out further possible written tasks beyond those originally intended. This has implications for individualised learning, in that the simulation provides a common context out of which particular written skills may arise and be developed.

The simulation material

Letter A

The Way Ahead with Wingair Associates

For the attention of the Chairman of Lowstead Residents' Committee

Here, indeed, is a dream come true: once upon a time Lowstead Airfield carried our lads into action against the might of Nazi Germany. Heroes and legends were born. However, the end of the war was the end of an era for Lowstead. No longer the metal chariots winging their way to victory; no longer the wit and banter of the air aces in the local inns and shops. When this important airfield was closed in 1945, a veritable limb of the community was lost to Lowstead. Wingair Associates hope to restore this historical feature to its former glory.

Picture your annual fete transformed into a well-supported and successful airshow with such crowd-pulling attractions as the Red Arrows Aerobatic team performing death-defying deeds on your very doorstep. This is no fantasy. With your support Lowstead Airport could rise, Phoenix-like, from the ashes. Wingair Associates have carefully researched the possibility of creating a small but select airfield on the sight of this gallant redundant war base. Though this concept may seem a little daring for your idyllic rural backwater, just examine some of the benefits, which could come your way with the advent of a thriving airport.

HERE ARE OUR PLANS

All existing runway space to be torn up and reasphalted; the main runway to be extended so as to accommodate small jets such as the Boeing 737 and British Aerospace's new prestigeous Airbus (Wingair Associates have ordered three of these beautiful machines); a small heliport to be built to cash in on the increasing demand for North Sea shuttle services; a small trading estate to be built in the immediate vicinity of the airport to attract further business to the area; an improved main road into Lowstead and the proposed airfield site.

All construction and roadworks should be completed by early 1986. All parties affected by the alterations have been approached and the majority have agreed to land sales.

WHAT WILL THIS MEAN TO LOWSTEAD?

All construction work, both road and building to be offered first to local firms (providing the tenders do not exceed our planned budget). All jobs created at the airport complex to be offered to the local work force (depending on skill). Also there may be many more jobs on offer with the inception of our new trading estate: a combination of office, warehouse, and light industry space.

All this and a share in the North Sea Oil bonanza, as many of these wealthy workers would regularly pass through the locality and come to value the true beauty of your picturesque market town.

We call on you to assist us in realizing a vision of wealth, colour and advanced technology. Say yes to Wingair Associates and find the way ahead.

Letter B

2 Marsh Cottages,
Lowstead
1/6/83

For the attention of the Chairman of Lowstead Residents' Committee

Dear Sir or Madam,

I am writing to you about the proposal of an airport for Lowstead. I shall come straight to the point and say that this will be a disaster for one and all in the area.

We read daily of all manner of air crashes. Why should we put the lives of our community on the line for a group of money-grabbing business men? Why should we pollute our atmosphere with these flying machines? Why should we deafen ourselves as these monsters land and take off on our doorsteps? We stand to gain nothing from this venture. No amount of new jobs can make up for the destruction and vandalism that this project will bring.

I enclose a map of the area which shows the proposals for the new airport. The number of trees and hedgerows that are to be uprooted will decimate the wildlife in our area. Wildlife, I might add, which has as much right as we to live peacefully on the planet. Hollows Pond is to be drained and filled as part of the operation. Hollows Pond is one of the few breeding grounds for the Raft Spider, an insect which is only kept from extinction by the existence of such ponds.

I would also like to point out that Mr. Jakes of Barny's Farm has agreed to sell off land to Wingair Associates for the development of the airfield. On this land are a pair of seventeenth century timber-framed cottages and a medieval tithe barn. These would be demolished in the event of planning permission being granted for the new airport. I live in one of these cottages and have rented it for the last fifteen years. What kind of world are we living in that would allow for the building of a monstrosity in a place of beauty and serenity?

I implore you to bring some of these items to the attention of your Residents' Committee at your next Annual General Meeting.

Your faithfully,
Cecilia Hawksworth (Widow).

LOWSTEAD AND SURROUNDS

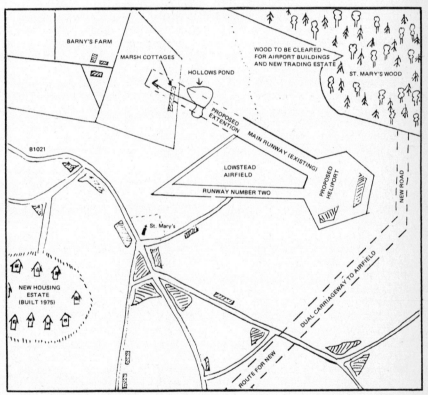

I have drawn in all the changes that the proposed airfield will bring.

Cecilia Hawksworth.

Letter C

The Farmers Arms
Lowstead
1/6/83

Dear (Your name),

Thank you for your letter regarding the Annual General Meeting of the Lowstead Residents' Committee.

I can confirm that our upstairs room will be free from 7.30 p.m. onwards on the 30th June. We will be able to provide light refreshment for the sum you mentioned and more substantial bar food will be available for those who wish to purchase it. A special bar will be set up in the upstairs room for your convenience. I will be more than happy to share the profit made on this bar.

I look forward to seeing you on the 30th. I would also like to take this opportunity to say that I fully support your Residents' Committee and am always at your service.

Yours sincerely,

Archie Lever (landlord).

Bibliography

APU (Assessment of Performance Unit, Department of Education and Science) (1978). *Language Performance*. London, HMSO.

APU (1981). *Language Performance in Schools*, Primary Survey Report no. 1. London, HMSO.

APU (1982). *Language Performance in Schools*, Secondary Report no. 1. London, HMSO.

APU (1983a). *Language Performance in Schools*, Primary Survey Report no. 2. London, HMSO.

APU (1983b). *Language Performance in Schools*, Secondary Report no. 2. London, HMSO.

APU (1983c). *Summary Report No. 13. Second Secondary Language Survey*. London, HMSO.

APU (1984). *Language Performance in Schools*, 1982 Secondary Survey Report. London, HMSO.

Augustine, D. (1981). 'Geometrics and Words: Linguistics and Philosophy: and Model of the Composing Process', *College English, 43* (3), pp. 221–31.

Bacon, F. (1876). *Essays*, ed. R. Whately. London, Longman & Green.

Barnes, D. (1976). *From Communication to Curriculum*. Harmondsworth, Penguin.

Barnsley, G. and Wilkinson, A. (1981). 'The Development of Moral Judgments in Children's Writing', *Educational Review, 33* (1).

Beard, R. (1984). *Children's Writing in the Primary School*. London, Hodder and Stoughton.

Bell, V. (1953). *On Learning the English Tongue*. London, Faber.

Bennett, B. (1983). 'Writers and their writing, 15 to 17' in Freedman, Pringle and Yalden (1983).

Bennett, B. (1985). 'Writer's in their place', in Wilkinson (1986).

Bennett, B. *et al.* (1977–9), Writing Research Project, University of Western Australia, English Dept. Eleven case studies edited variably by Bennett, B., Bowes, D., Sooby, A., Stone, J., Walker, A.

Bereiter, C. (1980). 'Development in Writing' in Gregg and Steinberg (1980).

Bidwell, J. (1985). 'Affective Aspects of Adolescent Writing at 9, 13, and 17', unpublished MA dissertation, University of East Anglia School of Education, Norwich.

Biggs, J. (forthcoming). 'Student Approaches to Learning and Essay Writing' in Schmeck, R. K. (ed.), *Learning Styles and Learning Strategies*. New York, Plenum Press.

Bobrow, D. and Collins, A. (eds.) (1975). *Representation and understanding*. Academic Press.

Bradley, L. and Bryant, P. (1983). 'Psychological Strategies and the Development of Reading and Writing' in Martlew (1983).

Britton, J., Martin, L. and Rosen, H. (1966). *Multiple Marking of Compositions*. HMSO.

Britton, J., Burgess, T., Martin, N., McLeod, A. and Rosen, H. (1975). *The Development of Writing Abilities (11–18)*. London, Macmillan.

Britton, J. with Barrs, M. and Burgess, T. (1979), 'No, no Jeanette! A Reply to Jeanette Williams' Critique of the Schools Council Writing Research Project', *Language for Learning, 1* (1).

Bruner, J. S. (1966). *Towards a Theory of Instruction*. Cambridge, Mass. Harvard University Press.

Bruner, J. S. (1975). 'Language as an Instrument of Thought' in Davies (1975).

Bullock Report (1975). A Language for Life. London, HMSO.

Burgess, C. et al. (1973). Understanding Children Writing. Harmondsworth, Penguin.

Carlin, E. (1986). 'Writing Development: Theory and Practice', in Wilkinson (1986).

Chomsky, C. (1979). 'Approaching Reading through Invented Spelling' in Resnick, L. A. and Weaver, P. A. (eds.), Theory and Practice in Early Reading. Hillsdale, N.J., Lawrence Erlbaum Associates.

Clay, M. (1975). What did I write? Beginning Writing Behaviour. Auckland, Heinemann.

Clegg, A. B. (1964). The Excitement of Writing. London, Chatto and Windus.

Coleridge, S. T. (1912). Poetical Works, ed. E. H. Coleridge. Oxford, Oxford University Press.

Collerson, J. (1983). 'One Child and One Genre: Developments in Letter Writing' in Kroll, B. M. and Wells, G. (eds.), Explorations in the Development of Writing. New York, John Wiley and Sons.

Cooper, C. R. and Matsuhashi, A. (1983). 'A theory of the Writing Process' in Martlew (1983).

Cooper, C. R. and Odell, L. (eds.)(1977). Evaluating Writing: Describing, Measuring, Judging. National Council of Teachers of English, Urbana, Illinois.

Creber, J. W. P. (1964). Sense and Sensitivity. London, University of London Press.

Curtis, R. (1982). 'One Is Continually Arriving', paper in part-fulfilment of the requirements for PhD, Atlantic Institute, Halifax, Nova Scotia.

Davies, A. (ed.) (1975). Problems of Language and Learning. London, Heinemann.

Davis, D. F., Ford, A. M., McBridge, A. R. and Spicer, D. J. (1978). Towards a Taxonomy of Essay Functions. Australian International Press, for the Curriculum Development Centre, Canberra.

DES (1979). Aspects of Secondary Education in England. A survey by HM Inspectors of Schools. London, HMSO.

DES (1984). English from 5 to 16. Curriculum Matters 1. An HMI Series. London, HMSO.

Diederich, P. B., French, J. W. and Carlton, S. T. (1961). Factors in Judgment of Writing Ability, Research Bulletin RB 61–15. Princeton, N.J., Educational Testing Service.

Diederich, P. B., (1974). Measuring Growth in English. NCTE, National Council of Teachers of English. Urbana, Illinois.

Dixon, J. (1967). Growth through English. Oxford, Oxford University Press.

Dixon, J. and Stratta, L. (n.d.). 'Achievements in Writing at 16+. Staging points reached in narratives based on personal experiences. Obtainable L. Stratta, Faculty of Education, Birmingham University, B15 2TT.

Dixon, J. and Stratta, (1982a). 'Argument'. What Does It Mean to Teachers of English', English in Education, Vol. 16, pp. 41–53.

Dixon, J. and Stratta, L. (1982b). 'Achievements in Writing at 16+. Narrative based on imagined experiences. Obtainable L. Stratta, Faculty of Education, Birmingham University, B15 2TT.

Drabble, M. (1979). A Writer's Britain: Landscape in Literature. London, Thames and Hudson.

Dunlop, F. (1984). The Education of Feeling and Emotion. London, Allen and Unwin.

Eagleson, R. D. (ed.) (1982). English in the Eighties. Australian Association for the Teachers of English.

Emig, J. (1971). The Composing Processes of Twelfth Graders, NCTE Research Report 13. National Council for the Teaching of English, Urbana, Illinois.

Ferreiro, E. (1978a). The Relationship between Oral and Written Language: The Children's Viewpoints. New York, Ford Foundation.

Ferreiro, E. (1978b). 'What is Written in a Written Sentence: A Developmental Answer', Journal of Education, 160 (4), pp. 25–39.

Finlayson, D. S. (1951). 'The Reliability of the Marking of Essays', *British Journal of Educational Psychology, 21* (2), pp. 126–34.

Ford, B. (ed.) (1960). *Young Writers, Young Readers.* London, Hutchinson.

Forster, E. M. (1927). *Aspects of the Novel.* Harmondsworth, Penguin (1974 edn).

Fowler, J. H. (1932). *The Art of Teaching English.* London, Macmillan.

Freedle, R. (1979). *New Directions in Discourse Processing,* Vol. 2: *Advances in Discourse Processing.* New York, Ablex Publishing Co.

Freedman, A. and Pringle, I. (1984). 'Why Students Can't Write Arguments', *English in Education, 18* (2).

Freedman, A., Pringle, I. and Yalden, J. (eds.) (1983). *Learning to Write: First Language, Second Language.* London, Longman.

Gannon, P. (1985). *Assessing Writing. Principles and Practice of Marking Written English.* London, Arnold.

Gleason, J. B. (1977). 'Talking to Children: Some Notes on Feedback, in Snow, C. E. and Feguson, C. A., *Talking to Children: Language Input and Acquisition.* London, Cambridge University Press.

Goffman, E. (1969). *The Presentation of Self in Everyday Life.* London, Allen Lane.

Goodnow, J. (1977). *Children's Drawing.* London, Fontana/Open Books, 1977.

Graves, D. H. (1982). 'Patterns of Child Control of the Writing Process' in Eagleson (1982).

Graves, D. H. (1983). 'The Growth and Development of First Grade Writers' in Freedman *et al.* (1983).

Gregg, L. W. and Steinberg, E. R. (eds.) (1980). *Cognitive Processes in Writing.* Hillsdale, N.J., Lawrence Erlbaum Associates.

Gurrey, P. (1954). *The Teaching of Written English.* London, Longman.

Haaf, R. A. and Bell, R. Q. (1967). 'A Facial Dimension in Visual Discrimination by Human Infants, *Child Development, 38,* pp. 893–9.

Halliday, M., Strevens, P. and McIntosh, D. (1964). *The Linguistic Sciences and Language Teaching.* London, Longman.

Hardy, B. (1968). 'Towards a Poetics of Fiction: An Approach through Narrative in Meek *et al.* (1977).

Hardy, B. (1975). *Tellers and Listeners.* London, Athlone Press.

Harpin, W. S. *et al.* (1973). *Social and Educational Influences on Children's Acquisition of Grammar: A Study of Writing Development in the Junior School.* SSRC Research Report.

Harpin, W. S. (1976). *The Second 'R': Writing Development in the Junior School.* London, George Allan & Unwin.

Harris, R. J. (1962). 'An Experimental Enquiry into the Function and Value of Formal Grammar', unpublished PhD thesis, University of London.

Harris, R. J. (1965). 'The Only Disturbing Feature', *Use of English, 16* (3).

Harrison, B. T. (1979). 'The Learner as Writer: Stages of Growth', *Language for Learning, 1* (2).

Harrison, B. T. (1983). *Learning Through Writing: Stages of Growth in English.* Windsor, NFER–Nelson.

Hartog, P. (1907). *The Writing of English.* Oxford, Oxford University Press.

Hartog, P. and Rhodes, E. C. (1935). *An Examination of Examinations.* London, Macmillan.

Hayes, P. and Flower, L. S. (1980). 'Identifying the Organisation of Writing Processes' in Gregg and Steinberg (1980).

Heath, W. G. (1962). 'Library-centred English', *Educational Review, 14* (2).

Hegginbotham, G. (1964). *Mirror, Mirror.* Privately printed.

Helm, J. (1967). *Essays in the Verbal and Visual Arts.* Seattle, University of Washington Press.

HMI, (n.d.) *Bullock Revisited: Discussion Paper by HMI. DES*, Room 1/27, Elizabeth House, York Road, London, SE1 7PH.

HMSO (1921). *The Teaching of English in England.*

Holbrook, D. (1961). *English for Maturity.* London, Cambridge University Press.

Hourd, M. (1949). *The Education of the Poetic Spirit.* London, Heinemann.

Hourd, M. and Cooper, G. (1959). *Coming Into Their Own.* London, Heinemann.

Hunt, K. W. (1965). 'Grammatical Structures Written at Three Grade Levels' NATE Research Report no. 3. National Council of Teachers of English, Urbana, Illinois.

Hurst, P. H. and Peters, R. S. (1970). *The Logic of Education.* London, Kegan Paul.

Inglis, F. (1969). *The Englishness of English Teaching.* London, Longman.

Jakobson, R. (1960). 'Concluding Statement: Linguistics and Poetics' in Sebeok (1960).

Jones, A., and Mulford, J. (eds)(1971). *Children Using Language.* London, Cambridge University Press.

Jones, R. M. (1968). *Fantasy and Feeling in Education.* New York, Harper, Colophon Books.

Kalmer, B. and Kilmarr, G. (1983). 'Looking at What Children Can Do' in Kroll and Wells (1983).

Kell, J. (1984). 'The Early Development of Discursive Writing', unpublished MA dissertation, University of East Anglia School of Education, Norwich.

Kernan, K. (1977). 'Semantic and Expressive Elaboration in Children's narratives' in Ervin-Tripp S. and Mitchell-Kernan C. (eds.) *Child Discourse*, New York, Academic Press.

King, R. (1979). 'Some-one's Being Silly', *Language for Learning, 1* (1).

Kirby, D. R. and Kantor, J. (1983). 'Towards a Theory of Developmental Rhetoric' in Freedman *et al.* (1983).

Kress, G. (1982). *Learning to Write.* Routledge and Kegan Paul.

Kroll, B. M., Kroll, D. L., and Wells, C. G. (1980). 'Researching Children's Writing Development', *Language for Learning, 2* (2).

Kroll, B. M. and Wells, G. (eds.) (1983). *Explorations in the Development of Writing.* New York and London, John Wiley and Sons.

Kulsdom, B. (1985). 'Moral Development in the Writing of Adolescents', study in part-fulfilment of MA requirements, University of East Anglia School of Education, Norwich.

Labov, W. (1977). *Language in the Inner City. Studies in the Black English Vernacular.* Oxford, Blackwell.

Labov, W., and Waletsky, J. (1967). 'Narrative Analysis. Oral Versions of Personal Experience' in Helm (1967).

Langton, M. (1961). *Let the Children Write.* London, Longman.

Larkin, P. (ed.) (1973). *Oxford Book of Twentieth Century English Verse.* London, Oxford University Press.

Lewis, C. S. (1977). 'On Stories' in Meek *et al.* (1977).

Lloyd-Jones, R. (1977). 'Primary Trait Scoring' in Cooper and Odell (1978).

Loban, W. (1963). *The Language of Elementary School Children.* National Council of Teachers of English, Urbana, Illinois.

Loban, W. (1976). *Language Development: Kindergarten through Grade Twelve.* National Council of Teachers of English, Urbana, Illinois.

Lowe, G. R. (1972). *The Growth of Personality.* Harmondsworth, Penguin.

Lyman, R. L. (1929). *Summary of Investigations Relating to Grammar, Language and Composition.* Supplementary Educational Monographs, no. 36, University of Chicago.

Mackay, D., Thompson, B. and Schaub, P. (1970). *Breakthrough to Literacy.* Teachers Book. London, Longman.

Maccauley, W. J. (1947) 'The difficulty of Grammar', *British Journal of Educational Psychology, 17*, (pp. 153–62.

Mandler, J. and Johnson, N. S. (1977). 'Remembrance of Things Parsed: Story Structure and Recall', *Cognitive Psychology, 8* pp. 111–81.

Marshall, C. (1985). 'The Hastings County Writing Programme', paper presented at the International Writing Convention, University of East Anglia, Norwich.

Martin, N. (1971). 'What Are They Up To? in Jones and Mulford (1971).

Martin, N., D'Arcy, P., Newton, B., and Parker, R. (1976). *Writing and Learning Across the Curriculum, 11–16*. Ward Lock.

Martlew, M. (1983). 'Problems and Difficulties: Cognitive and Communicative Aspects of Writing Development', in Martlew (ed.) (1983).

Martlew, M. (ed). (1983). *The Psychology of Written Language.* John Wiley and Sons (published in New York, 1981).

Meek, M., Warlow, A. and Barton, G. (eds.) (1977). *The Cool Web. The Pattern of Children's Reading.* London, The Bodley Head.

Minovi, R. (1976). *Early Reading and Writing.* London, Allen & Unwin.

Moffett, J. (1968). *Teaching the Universe of Discourse.* Boston, Houghton, Mifflin Co.

Newson, J. and Newson, E. (1975). 'Intersubjectivity and the transmission of culture', *Bulletin of the British Psychological Society, 28.*

Ontario Ministry of Education (1982). *Focus on Writing.* Curriculum Ideas for Teachers.

Paramour, S. E. (1983). 'The Development of Narrative Writing in Students of Seven to Thirteen', unpublished MEd thesis. University of East Anglia School of Education, Norwich.

Paramour, S. E. and Wilkinson, A. M.(1985). 'The Disruption of the Probable: An Aspect of Narrative Writing 3–13', *Language Arts, 62* (4).

Peel, E. A. (1956). *The Psychological Basis of Education.* Edinburgh, Oliver and Boyd.

Peel, E. A. (1960). *The Pupil's Thinking.* London, Oldbourne Book Co.

Peel, E. A. (1971). *The Nature of Adolescent Judgment.* London, Staples Press.

Poole, M. (1983). 'Socioeconomic Status and Written Language' in Martlew(1983).

Pringle, I. and Freedman, A. (1984). 'A Comparative Study in Writing Abilities in Two Modes at Grade 5, 8 and 12 level', Department of Linguistics, Carleton University, Ottawa.

Protherough, R. (1983). *Encouraging Writing.* London, Methuen.

Purves, A. C. and Takala, S. (1982). 'An International Perspective on the Evaluation of Written Composition', *Evaluation in Education, 5*, pp. 205–370.

Pym, D. (1956). *Free Writing.* London, University of London Press.

Rice, J. M. (1903–4). 'Educational Research: The Results of a Test in Language and English', *Forum, 35*, pp. 209–93, 440–53.

Rumelhart, E. (1975). 'Notes on a Schema for Stories', in Bobrow and Collins (1975).

Sanders, N. M. (1966). *Classroom Questions: What Kind?* New York, Harper and Row.

Scardamalia, M. and Bereiter, C. (1983). 'The Development of Evaluative Diagnostic and Remedial Capabilities in Children's Composing' in Martlew (1983).

Scholes, R. and Kellogg, R. (1966). *The Nature of Narrative.* Oxford, Oxford University Press.

Schonell, F. J. and Schonell, F. E. (1948). *Diagnostic and Attainment Testing.* Edinburgh, Oliver and Boyd.

Sebeok, T. A. (ed.) (1960). *Style in Language.* Cambridge, Mass., Massachusetts Institute of Technology.

Secord, D. F. and Backman, C. W. (1974). *Social Psychology.* Tokyo, McGraw-Hill/ Kogakusha Ltd.

Shafer, R. E. (1983). 'A Child's Power to Share: The Development of a Personal Experience Model of the Writing Process' in Kroll and Wells (1983).

Smith, R. (1983). 'The Revision of Children's Writing in Small Groups', unpublished Advanced Certificate dissertation, University of East Anglia School of Education, Norwich.

Spencer, E. (1983). *Writing Matters Across the Curriculum*. SCER (Scottish Council for Research in Education), 15 St. John Street, Edinburgh, EH8 8JR.

Squire, J. R. and Applebee, R. K. (1969). *Teaching of English in the United Kingdom*. National Council of Teachers of English, Urbana, Illinois.

Stein, N. and Glenn, C. (1979). 'Analysis of Story Comprehension in Elementary School Children' in Freedle (1979).

Sternglass, M. (1981). 'Assessing Reading, Writing And Reasoning', *College English*, March.

Sternglass, M. (1982). 'Applications of the Wilkinson Model of Writing Maturity to college Writing', *College Composition and Communication*, *33* (2).

Sternglass, M. (1985). 'The Relationship of Task Demands to Cognitive Level', paper presented at the International Writing Convention, University of East Anglia, Norwich, Easter.

Stratta, L., Dixon, J. and Wilkinson, A. (1973). *Patterns of Language*. London, Heinemann.

Swan, M. (1980). 'The Dartmouth Children's Writing Project', unpublished report, Nova Scotia Teachers College, Truro, N.S.

Taylor, G. (1986). 'The Development of Style in Children's Fictional Narrative', in Wilkinson (1986).

Thomas, D. (1967). *Collected Poems 1934–1952*. London, Dent.

Thompson, D. (1964). Forward, in Clegg (1964).

Thompson, J. (1980). *The Writing Process*. Curriculum Development Centre, Canberra, Australia.

Thornton, G. (1980). *Teaching Writing: The Development of Written Language Skills*. London, Arnold.

Vigar, M. (1985). 'Cognitive Development in the Work of Older Writers with Particular Reference to the Writing of Argument by Students in a College of Further Education', study in part-fulfilment of MA requirements, University of East Anglia School of Education, Norwich.

Walshe, W. (1981). *Every Child Can Write*. Primary English Teachers Association, Australia.

Whitehead, F. (1966). *The Disappearing Dais*. London, Chatto and Windus.

Whitehead, F. (1977). 'What's the Use, Indeed?', *Use of English*, *29* (2), pp. 15–22.

Wilcock, E. (1985). 'Crediton in the Classroom', study in part-fulfilment of MA requirements, University of East Anglia School of Education, Norwich.

Wilkinson, A. M. (1965). *Spoken English*, Educational Review Occasional Publications no. 2. University of Birmingham.

Wilkinson, A. M. (1971). *Foundations of Language*. Oxford, Oxford University Press.

Wilkinson, A. M. (1975). *Language and Education*. Oxford, Oxford University Press.

Wilkinson, A. M. (1982). 'The Quality of Writing', *Education 3–13*, *10* (2).

Wilkinson, A. M. (1983a). 'Assessing Language Development' in Freedman *et al.* (1983).

Wilkinson, A. M. (1983b). 'The Quality of Feeling', keynote paper at CCTE Conference, Montreal, 1983.

Wilkinson, A. M. (1985a). 'Writing' in Bennett, N. and Desforges, C. (eds.), *Recent Advances in Classroom Research*, British Journal of Educational Psychology Monograph Series no. 2. Edinburgh, Scottish Academic Press.

Wilkinson, A. M. (1985b). 'I communicate, therefore I am', *Educational Review*, *37* (1).

Wilkinson, A. M. (ed.) (1986). *The Writing of Writing*. Milton Keynes, Open University Press.

Wilkinson, A. M., Barnsley, G., Hanna, P. and Swan, M. (1980). *Assessing Language Development*. Oxford, Oxford University Press.

Wilkinson, A. M., Barnsley, G., Hanna, P. and Swan, M. (1982). 'The Development of Writing' in Adams, A. (ed.), *New Directions in English Teaching.* Lewes, Falmer Press (originally published in *English in Education,* 13 (3) (Autumn 1980).

Wilkinson, A. M., Barnsley, G., Hanna, P. and Swan, M. (1984). 'Towards a Comprehensive Model of Writing Development' in Kroll and Wells (1983).

Wilkinson, A. M. and Hanna, P. (1980). 'The Development of Style in Children's Writing', *Educational Review, 32* (2).

Wilkinson, A. M., Stratta, L. and Dudley, P. (1974). *The Quality of Listening.* London, Macmillan.

Wilkinson, A. M. and Wilkinson, E. (1978). 'The Development of Language in the Middle Years', *English in Education, 12* (1).

Williams, J. T. (1977). *Learning to Write, or Writing to Learn?* Slough, NFER Publishing Company.

Wills, D. M. (1977). 'The Ordinary Devoted Mother and Her Blind Baby', *The Psychoanalytic Study of the Child, 34.*

Wiseman, S. (1949). 'The Marking of English Composition in Grammar School Selection', *British Journal of Educational Psychology, 19* (3) pp. 200–9.

Wittstein, S. S. (1983). 'Four Case Studies: An Analysis and Assessment of Inner-City High School Student Writing Using Three Measures of the Wilkinson Model of Writing Maturity', unpublished thesis for the Degree of Doctor of Education, University of Cincinnati.

Wordsworth, W. (1800). Preface to the Lyrical Ballads, in W. M. Merchant (ed.), *Wordsworth, Poetry and Prose.* London, Hart-Davies.

Worsley, G. (1983). 'The Quality of Feeling in the Writing of Older Adolescents', unpublished MA dissertation, University of East Anglia School of Education, Norwich.

Index